PRASE FOR ▋▋▋▋▋

Paul's book hits key lessons that ▋
– dream big, play with purpose a
lenge, and bring your best to everything you do.

—NFL Hall of Famer Ronnie Lott

This book is a must read for young athletes and their parents on how to succeed in sports, but more importantly, in life.

—National Championship Coach John Robinson

Far too many athletes (as well as their families and fans) are preoccupied with championship trophies and titles, but have lost touch with what matters most: *championship* lives. Paul, in his insightful and inspiring work, reminds us of this timeless truth: that what you are *believing* and who you are *becoming* are the essential ingredients to elite performance and extraordinary lives.

—Life Coach & Podcaster Dr. Michael Brown

Paul's book is a perfect reflection of his arc as a person: authentic, pragmatic, and great to be around. My career has involved working with high performance individuals in athletics and business, and few possess the clarity of mind, and most importantly, the commitment to a pursuit of personal knowledge and kindness that Paul demonstrates. Paul's book also shows the limits of relying on any one particular identity (athlete, founder, etc). His story helps to show that our self will always be greater and more precious than our accomplishments.

—Neuroscientist / USC Lecturer of
Entrepreneurship Dr. Glenn Fox

THRU THE
TUNNEL

TRUE STORIES OF SPORTS AND
LIFE THAT EMPOWER YOUR SPIRIT

PAUL MCDONALD
WITH JACK BARIC

Thru the Tunnel: True Stories of Sports and Life That Empower Your Spirit
Published by GameChange
Los Angeles, CA

ISBN 978-0-578-30965-1

AUTOBIOGRAPHY / Sports

Cover and interior design by Victoria Wolf, wolfdesignandmarketing.com, copyright owned by GameChange.
Photos by John Mattera.

This book is dedicated to those seeking a more fulfilled life and the people who want to create a better world.

CONTENTS

PREFACE

BY JACK BARIC

WHAT DOES A QUARTERBACK look like?

Sometime around 2010, I watched a documentary film about the college football rivalry between Ohio State and Michigan, and it sparked an idea. It was a good film, but in my opinion the rivalry between my alma mater, USC, and our crosstown rival, UCLA, is way better. In our rivalry, we share a city. So the gameday drive to the Memorial Coliseum or the Rose Bowl to watch the Trojans and Bruins duke it out for LA bragging rights might include a husband and a wife, a father and a son, two sisters, or the co-owners of a company, who on this day are mortal enemies because one of them attended UCLA and the other USC.

I had the perfect title for the film: *A City Divided*. Now, I just had to figure out a way to get it made! I mentioned the idea to my buddy, Mike Setlich, and he instantly said, "You've got to meet Paul McDonald. He can help." Paul was the radio game analyst for USC football games and one of the legends of the university. He was a former All-American quarterback and started on the 1978 Trojans national championship team, which included superstars such as Ronnie Lott, Marcus Allen, Charles White, and Anthony Munoz.

Mike set up a meeting for me to pitch the idea to Paul, and we agreed to hook up at the San Pedro Brewing Company for a beer. The establishment is owned by my friend James Brown, a UCLA alum—and so two Trojans would connect at a Bruin bar to discuss a rivalry film between the schools. Perfect. When I asked Mike how I would know who Paul was, he replied, "You'll know. He looks like a quarterback." Uh, okay.

I sat in a booth at the bar with an eye on the door, and I kind of chuckled when Paul walked in. A shaft of sunlight might as well have been streaking down through the clouds to form a halo over this guy's head! He sauntered in sporting a million-dollar smile and a calm aura of confidence that only a select few people on this planet possess. He was a quarterback. I waved Paul over and, as he slid into the booth, his infectious positive spirit immediately took over. This dude was the golden boy!

I explained the film idea to Paul, and he seemed somewhat interested. However, he sparked up considerably when I added that we could use the film to bring supporters of the two universities together to raise money for a good cause. We agreed right then that we'd find a way to get the film made and that a charity would benefit from the red carpet premiere. What I learned that day about Paul has held true for all of the years I've been his friend—nothing motivates him more than helping others. He liked the film idea, but he loved that we'd be doing it to help people.

A few days later, Paul ran into his good friend Barry Hoeven, and we found our charity. Barry had just recently launched Kure It, a non-profit dedicated to raising funds to fight "orphan" cancers. These are cancers that pharmaceutical companies don't address because they don't have a big enough population of patients to provide a return on the massive investment that researching cures requires. Barry started the charity because he was diagnosed with kidney cancer and quickly found out that there were almost no treatments available to him. Kidney cancer is one of many orphan cancers that only get researched through government or non-profit funding.

Our documentary film, *A City Divided,* launched a campaign, "Rivals United for a Kure," with the premiere of the film at LA Live. The event was such a hit that for a number of years afterward, fans, players, and coaches from both teams gathered for an annual game week gala that benefited the cause. To date, the campaign has netted over $3 million, which has been donated to UCLA and USC's amazing cancer research hospitals. Barry courageously fought cancer for over fifteen years, chaired many of the Rivals United events, but sadly died from the disease in 2016.

Throughout the process of making the film and planning events for Rivals United, Paul and I became great friends, and I had the pleasure of getting to know his beautiful wife, Allyson, and their wonderful family. I also got to meet scores of Paul's buddies in the real estate industry. Some of the events for Rivals United were hosted at these friends' palatial homes that were honestly so spectacular you'd think you were on the set of a movie. All of this, plus Paul's unwavering positive attitude, contributed to the aura of the golden boy quarterback who didn't have a worry in the world.

Maybe not.

As I got to know Paul better, he shared with me that there was a time in his life when he was not happy and that things needed to change. Honestly, many people who outwardly seem to have a great life are not happy on the inside and will pour another glass of wine or vodka and keep grinding through the rest of their lives in quiet despair.

Paul decided he wanted more.

He threw himself full force into becoming a student of both life—and of himself. As he learned more and more, Paul discovered the joy within himself that had been previously lacking, and his natural inclination to help people motivated him to share his newfound knowledge. He taught a class at USC and would eagerly explain to anybody who would listen the various life principles that he had learned.

I would tease Paul that people saw him as a quarterback and not a Tony Robbins, but the more I learned from him, the more I appreciated his perspective on the things we were discussing. It also made me start thinking about how many people are sleepwalking through life with little joy or direction. I'm convinced that people's lack of hope for a better life is one of the reasons there is so much anger and unhappiness in our country. We live in extremely divided times where people have become far more inclined to point their fingers at others as the source of their unhappiness rather than looking inward to find a personal path to a more joyful life.

Paul had a big impact on me and how I viewed life, especially in how to deal with adversity. We often found ourselves using sports analogies to explain life principles. It's just what came natural to us. We both love sports and especially the many lessons that can be learned from playing and being on a team. We're not the only ones. Millions of people will tell you that sports played a major role in helping them develop strong character, solid work habits, and being a great teammate. We started thinking, what if we created a platform where athletes, scientists, and professionals could use sports stories as a way of teaching important life lessons?

Our hundreds of hours of conversations turned into the blueprint for GameChange, a company we have co-founded to empower people through sports. GameChange creates and distributes daily content on various social media platforms. Our website includes mindset, nutrition, and fitness classes, and we publish sports-themed books that include all the wonderful life lessons that athletics can provide. You are holding our first product in your hands.

We hope you enjoy the book, and we invite you to join our GameChangeNation community where we will embark on learning together, supporting each other, and having a blast playing the sports that we love.

MY HALFTIME
ADJUSTMENT

THE MIRROR DOESN'T LIE. In the spring of 2008, it was early one morning when I stumbled into my Las Vegas hotel room after another night of drinking and caught a glimpse. I didn't like what I saw in front of me.

On the surface, nobody had a better life than me. I played quarterback at the University of Southern California, where I got to fling footballs around the coliseum on sunny fall afternoons in front of thousands of cheering fans. My Trojan team won the national championship during my junior year, and I was fortunate enough to be named All-American quarterback as a senior.

This was followed up by an eight-year career in the NFL, which began with the Cleveland Browns. My time with the Browns was during an era when the team was competing head-to-head with the Pittsburgh Steelers for AFC Central Division championships and regularly making the playoffs. Let me tell you something; very few fans in professional sports have more passion than Cleveland's, and playing in front of the Dawg Pound was awesome! I later got to play for the Dallas Cowboys and legendary coach Tom Landry. This is the stuff that kids playing backyard football only dream of, and it was my life.

On a personal level, I had a good second career in business, a nice home, an amazing wife, and four incredible children. It would be easy to look at me and think there goes the

Golden Boy, not a problem in sight. So, why didn't it feel that way on the inside?

This is a story that has played out countless times with former athletes. They get to live their dream by playing a sport they love, but they continue to hold onto it long after their playing days are over. It is a challenge to find a purpose, a career that can fill the huge void created by a life without sports.

I filled the void with parties. My drug of choice was vodka and soda, with a splash of cranberry—and my ready and willing posse were my numerous compadres in the commercial real estate industry. Like many professions, the real estate business is built on relationships. There are numerous conferences all over the nation, but Las Vegas is easily the favorite spot to meet, mingle, and do some business.

The night I found myself looking in the mirror, my buzz fading, and the inevitable hangover beginning to creep in, something essential within me happened—I awakened. Even though the fog of too many drinks was still clouding my mind, a strong streak of clarity had cut through. I realized this was becoming too much. I had begun to lose my way. The pool parties at the Hard Rock Hotel, or being on the VIP list at the MGM, were taking me away from the things in life that are far more important.

I had been taking full advantage of the social way the real estate industry operates to fill my need for having the fun that I missed out on earlier in my life when I was a dedicated athlete with a young family to take care of. I mentioned earlier that vodka was my drug of choice, but truthfully it was seeking the next fun night out, drinking with my friends, that I was getting addicted to. On the outside, everyone saw fun guy Paul, always willing to chase the next great party with you, but honestly, the next day's hangover was a more accurate description of how I felt on the inside after the music had stopped and everyone went home.

Things were not great, and I didn't even know why. So, I frequently numbed myself thinking everything would feel better the next day. I did not know this at the time, but I was searching. I was searching for internal peace and a renewed passion. And I was searching in the wrong places. I had to change because if I continued operating in this party-machine manner, it would result in my own destruction. I was headed down a path that was unsustainable. A path that was not right for me. A path that was not my destiny.

My current playbook was becoming devoid of the things that would allow me to live a successful and joyful life. It was time to make a halftime adjustment.

I decided to find the true Paul—not the former football player, the son, brother, father, husband, or friend. Not the business executive, not the sports announcer. I wanted to discover what was underneath all those masks that I wore every day. I needed to clear my head and do a deep dive into Paul 101.

I decided to really take the time to go inward, clear away the cobwebs, and discover what was inside. Who was I? What made me tick? What did I want to do with my life? How did I want to live it? I'll be honest. It was scary. What if I didn't like what I saw? How would I deal with that?

All these things were swirling around my head, but the fact that I even wanted to do a thorough self-evaluation was evidence that I was headed in the right direction. However, I couldn't just go sit in my living room or close the door of my office. I would need adequate time, space, and quiet, to honestly evaluate my life and where I wanted it to go. I decided that I needed a weekend away, all by myself, with no distractions and plenty of time to think and maybe even feel. I decided I would drive to Indian Wells for a long weekend of introspection.

Easy enough, right? Imagine walking up to your wife and saying, "Hey, hon, I'm going to the desert this weekend to work on myself." Uh, yeah.

It took a lot to convince my wife, Allyson, why I needed to go on a personal retreat alone. She had to be thinking, "Something must be wrong with him" because this was the first time I had embarked on such a journey. I give her an enormous amount of credit because it took courage for her to let me go find myself. Why? One of the great fears in life is fear of change. What if I came back different? What if she didn't like the new Paul? What if, because of this trip, we grew apart? These were thoughts roaming around in her imagination, for sure. But she agreed to let me go, and I love her for it.

As I drove along the 10 freeway toward the desert, I had this sinking feeling of doubt and loneliness. Was this a mistake? I was leaving my wife and family behind on a journey of self-discovery, but I was now more scared than ever of what I would find. This fear prevents a lot of people stuck in a rut from trying and making changes that could lead to a happier and more fulfilling life.

For so many people, going through life in a trance is preferable to the risk of asking the necessary questions of yourself that require brutally honest answers. You must dig deep and be willing to not only discover the things that you like about yourself but admit where you have not lived to your full potential. As the desert drew nearer, these were the fears that I grappled with.

I think it is okay to say that I am proud of myself. I did not get into the Indian Wells vacation home and turn on ESPN. I went to work. I hunkered down from Friday through Sunday, eight to ten hours a day, reading books, listening to CDs, and journaling to rediscover who I was. I began to answer these life-changing questions. I learned so much about myself that weekend; the experience resulted in a new path, outlook, and vision for my life.

Undoubtedly, I would not have written this book if I had not paid attention to the fact that I was off course. It is taking that first step—facing our fears—that allows us to move through them to a new state of being. It is undoubtedly scary, and it takes commitment, but please believe me when I tell you, it is something that you can do, and as you move through the process, you will start to realize that better days are within your grasp.

One of the things I learned is how much being on a team and serving others meant to me. I learned so many great life lessons while playing sports, so *Thru the Tunnel* includes many sports stories that nicely illustrate those lessons I learned and philosophies I developed, which have greatly enhanced my life.

The book includes eleven principles that I believe provide great examples for how to live life to the fullest. My hope is that you will benefit from some of these takes on life, so you, too, can be transformed into the person you were designed to be—one with purpose, one who is passionate about life, one who gives more than receives, one who is grateful, one who is at peace with themselves—a true success!

THE ELEVEN

I. KNOW YOURSELF
Dive inward to discover yourself, your
passions, and your greatest strengths

II. BELIEVE
Believe you are a miracle and
that change is possible

III. BE AUTHENTIC
Strive to be your best authentic self,
not someone else's version

IV. GO FOR IT!
Take action and have trust in the flow of life

V. GRIT
View your challenges as experiences that
make you stronger and help you grow

VI. COURAGE
Have the courage to be vulnerable
and face your challenges

VII. FORGIVE

Let go of all failures and mistakes—
forgive yourself and others

VIII. BE CONSCIOUS

Stay present and be mindful of all you think, say, and do

IX. INNER PEACE

See the abundance that life offers and
have gratitude for all you receive

X. MENTORSHIP

We all need support and encouragement—find a mentor, be a mentor

XI. A FULFILLED LIFE

Live life with purpose—love, be compassionate, and serve others

I. KNOW YOURSELF

Dive inward to discover yourself, your passions, and your greatest strengths

WHO AM I?

HOW CAN YOU BELIEVE IN YOURSELF if you don't know yourself?

Marta Vieira da Silva had no problem figuring out who she was. Famously known in the world of soccer by only her first name, Marta was born to be a soccer player. She is considered by many to be the queen of soccer. This Brazilian player has scored more Women's World Cup goals (seventeen), than any other player in the history of the sport and has been named the FIFA Female World Player of the Year six times, three more than the next highest player.[1]

It didn't come easy for Marta. She grew up poor. Her father left their home when Marta was just a baby, leaving her mom to raise four kids by herself. All the children had to chip in to help pay the household bills. At the age of seven, Marta started to work, selling ice cream and fruit at street fairs. She split the money she earned, giving half to her mom to pay the electric bill. The other half she saved to buy a pair of sneakers so that she could play soccer.[2]

Marta had a passion for soccer from a very young age and honed her skills playing on the streets with the boys from her neighborhood. Although she was an amazing player, Marta had the burden of being a girl playing a boys' game. In Brazil, the game was not seen as something that girls should be doing. Women were banned from the sport from 1941 to 1979 because it was not considered to be in their nature to play.

Although the restriction had been lifted by the time Marta was born in 1986, there were still very limited opportunities for young ladies in soccer. With no organized girls teams to join, Marta signed up with a boys team at the age of ten, the only girl on the squad. She was such a crafty dribbler that nobody could get the ball from her, and she emerged as one of the best players in the league.[3]

Despite Marta being a star on the field, she still suffered discrimination from other players. They would give her disparaging nicknames and ask her why she kept insisting on coming around. Even her brother and aunts would question Marta's mom for allowing her to play with the boys. However, Marta was not deterred.

With all the obstacles placed in front of her, from growing up in deep poverty to gender discrimination, Marta knew in her heart what she wanted to do and who she wanted to be. She did not let other people define who she was. Her drive to play the game she loved was so great that she was willing to absorb the insults and step onto a field where she was told she didn't fit in. Ironically, she became the queen of the very place she was once told she didn't belong.[4]

Many people haven't developed a strong conviction about who they are and what they want to do. This is especially true for teens and young adults. Not everybody is blessed with the sense of direction that Marta had, which tells them early on that they want to be a soccer player, an astronaut, or a businessperson. That's completely normal and fine.

As you are figuring out what you want to do, it's important to try different things to see what you enjoy and where your innate gifts might lie. Through the process of elimination, you can also learn the things that don't inspire you. It's okay not to fit in with what everyone else around you is doing. Trying to keep up with the Joneses will always create the worst kind of misery.

Everyone is on their own path.

We all have a place at the table, and, as Marta proved, the best way to fit in is to be true to who you are, not who other people believe you should be. I can't think of a better person in the world who exhibits this quality of fitting in by just being their own authentic self than my daughter, Stephanie. In contrast to Marta, when it came to playing sports, Stephanie had a polar-opposite perspective.

In a family whose lives revolve around sports, Stephanie was not born to be an athlete. From my football career to youth, high school, and college sports for Stephanie's three brothers, it has been nonstop testosterone and competition in the McDonald house from the day she arrived. Sports is just what we do. My wife of thirty-nine years, Allyson, and I were even the proud golf champions of a local couples tournament at the club where we play!

Allyson and I tried our best to encourage Stephanie to take part in athletics. Allyson went so far as to learn soccer from scratch to be Stephanie's coach in a neighborhood co-ed league. Stephanie agreed to play because her mom would be the coach, but this only lasted about three weeks before she said, "no *más*." It wasn't her thing. We could not mold her into this sports-crazed athlete with a burning passion for competing. Winning a game was just not that important to Stephanie.

What mattered most to Steph were the personal relationships she developed with her friends. These relationships led her to enjoy dance as a youngster and to play field hockey in high school. She participated because it was fun, and she could spend more time with her girlfriends. It wasn't about the trophy or recognition from participating that motivated Stephanie. It was about being in the moment and enjoying the experience, which was such a relaxed and refreshing way to operate in the world compared to my perspective as a former athlete.

Stephanie was an outlier in the McDonald household. Her greatest role in contributing to our family was not to step in line with what the rest of us did. In finding her own way, Stephanie provided different perspectives that could help make the rest of us into more well-rounded and better individuals. As an example, something that took me well over fifty years to learn was her great quality of not taking life too seriously. I wish I learned that one a lot earlier!

Stephanie has a quirky sense of humor, which lightens the mood of every room she enters. When you combine these characteristics with a big dose of sensitivity and compassion for others, you can appreciate why she doesn't have the killer instinct most often required in high-level sports and why people want to be around her. These innate qualities helped Stephanie round out the rough male edges that developed in the household through all our years of competition.

Ironically, the key to my transition was discovering that, like Stephanie, I was more interested in developing relationships with people than in competing with them. I didn't realize how much her approach to life resonated with me until I began reflecting on the changes I made, which brought me the joy I was seeking.

Like Marta, I grew up with a laser-sharp focus on who I wanted to be. I wanted to be a football player—more specifically, a quarterback. In football, I played to win because that is the objective of the game. But that's not the reason I played. The position is what I fell in love with.

The quarterback position is arguably the most challenging job in all sports. The mental, physical, and emotional demands pushed me to the limit, which is why I was so intrigued with the game. You have to perform a skill, throwing the football, with ridiculous accuracy to a target moving twenty miles per hour or more downfield while under duress from massive guys charging full speed at you, hell-bent on knocking you to the ground. Oh, and by the way, you have four or five different receivers you can throw it to, and you must make the decision while moving backward in less than three seconds, or you're hit. Everyone associated with the team is looking to you to set the tone, lead, and provide the answers. I loved it!

I competed every day. Yes, other players pushed me, but I was really competing to do my best every time on the field. I was competing with myself by continually working on my craft, which was a never-ending process, much like life.

Sometimes we won, and sometimes we lost, but I never stopped working on improving because I loved playing quarterback so much. This is why it is so important to understand what the underlying motivations are that drive you, where your passion is, and where your natural gifts lie. If you have this personal knowledge and can express it in your career and job, you will enjoy your work much more and be a happier person.

In sports, like in life, it takes hard work and a strong will to be successful. You can often hear announcers say that a player willed his team to win. But the part that they don't typically explain is that most of the players they are referring to developed their strong will because they have a deep passion for what they are doing.

In football, I had the will, but I also had the heart, which took me to heights I could never have imagined. It all stemmed from the fact that I loved playing quarterback. It's not all cake and punch. For example, I did not like training camp. You would have to be a special kind of crazy to enjoy two-a-days in August in 100 degrees and 100 percent humidity. But you do the work because it allows you the chance to play a game that you love.

Football was awesome, but playing in the NFL has a short shelf life. I went from knowing exactly who I was to having very little idea of what to do next when my career was over. I am not alone. This is a massive challenge for many athletes.

You play sports your whole life, and then one day, you are told to "go join the real world." Like many athletes, I decided to get into business, put my head down, and will my way to a successful new career. No problem, right? Uh, big problem.

A lot of people get into a career that they don't enjoy, not because they have a love for the work, but because they think they can make enough money to survive or, even better, hit the jackpot. Their only underlying motivation is money. They apply a strong will to succeed and grind away at a job that they can't stand. Oftentimes the money does come rolling in, but they can't ignore the fact they are not happy and that unhappiness can manifest in many negative ways. That was me.

I transitioned to the business world when I was thirty years old, and I did not have the same sense of underlying motivations that I had for being a quarterback. I merely applied things I learned from football, like a great work ethic and tenacity, which worked for a while. I set goals. I showed up. I met and even exceeded my numbers, but I wasn't happy.

Notice I said numbers? Salespeople will tell you that they are most often judged by the number of dollars they bring in. I fell into the same trap as so many people in sales. It was all about the numbers. The numbers I could bring into the company. The numbers on my paycheck. The numbers I hoped to have in my bank account by a certain age. My job and my life were all about chasing numbers. I was lost. I might as well have been chasing ghosts.

This is the part of the story where you probably think I will tell you that I changed jobs to find my happiness. Guess again! The coolest thing is I did not change my career. All

I changed was my perspective on my job by diving within myself to discover why I was doing what I was doing!

All the answers you seek in life come from within. Give yourself the proper time to really think, to dive inward, and discover the things that make you tick. What makes you happy? What scares you? What causes are important to you? How can you help? What do you recall from childhood that you loved? That was painful? If you had a year to live and the freedom to do whatever you like, what would it be? Who would you want to do it with that year?

Ask yourself all of these questions and more. Become a student of yourself—and don't settle for a bachelor's degree; get a PhD! From this state, you will be able to cut through the clutter of life to tap into your (oftentimes guarded) innermost thoughts and feelings. You will start to understand what is important to you and what you can cast away. Focus your attention on what's most important.

Everybody has their own favorite ways to find quiet time and achieve this. It could be through journaling, walking in the park, strolling on a beach, or through yoga, prayer, or meditation. Whatever discipline serves you best to quiet the mind can work. So, feel free to be creative.

I decided that a trip to the desert reading, journaling, and listening to my soul would be my best way to find the quiet time that I needed to figure out where my unhappiness stemmed from.

On my drive to Indian Wells, I was feeling lost and full of self-doubt. It is important to understand that this process can be painful because past experiences or beliefs may bubble up to the surface. This is good news, so stay with it because you must move through any potential unpleasantness. Resist the temptation to quit. Once processed, a heavy load will be lifted from your being, and you will be free again! However, you may need guidance through these painful experiences, so don't hesitate to seek personal or professional assistance.

So what did my awakening in the desert teach me about myself? First and foremost, stop looking at the scoreboard. I stopped using hitting my numbers and making money as my sole motivation. I learned what was most important to me—connecting with people and helping them. I stopped selling and started listening. My meetings with people became all about what I could do to assist them—and it often had nothing to do with the products or services that my company offered. I built real relationships!

Incredibly, I became Stephanie, the McDonald outlier. I became focused on other people before myself, and it made all the difference. I was happier with my place at my company. I was happier with my place in society. I was happier with myself! It took me fifty years to discover what Stephanie knew as a young girl. The tough, competitive NFL player now had a heart just like his only daughter, and I loved it.

The most interesting aspect of my newfound approach to work and thinking of others first is the numbers began to increase to the point we were doing more business than ever before. Crazy, right?

It's in the letting go that we receive!

The trip to the desert was the first leg of a journey that goes on to this day. Honestly, the journey never ends, but that is a good thing because the more your curiosity grows and you learn more things about yourself and about life, the more passionate you become. The more I searched, the more engrossed in the process I became. I realized learning and being open to new ways of thinking and living is a lifetime process because we are here to grow and evolve.

No matter the level we are at when we come into existence on this planet, the objective is to improve, to grow, to be better each day. So, I realized the best way to be better was to really understand myself, know my strengths, weaknesses, limiting beliefs, the masks I wear, my desires, my true potential, and my destiny. There is no greater mission in life than to be open, honest, and completely transparent with ourselves about who we really are.

I urge you all to take off your mainstream blinders and find what's right for you. Think about it: in the mainstream of Brazil, soccer was once not for girls, and out of that emerged Marta, the global queen of soccer. Do not fear the opinions of others. Whether it be scientific, spiritual, or a combination of the two, find the best ways to discover the best of who you are and don't stop. Keep growing!

PERSONAL IDENTITY

WHAT MASK DO YOU WEAR?

Carey Price is an amazing goalie who has skated between the pipes for the Montreal Canadiens for thirteen seasons. In that time, he made the All-Star team numerous times, was voted best goalie at the 2014 Sochi Olympics (where he led team Canada to a gold medal), and was MVP of the NHL in 2015.[5]

At the conclusion of the 2015 season, Price was in Las Vegas for the NHL Awards, where he would win four trophies, including the aforementioned MVP. While at the MGM, Price played a low-key role in a hilarious prank video, which was made for the awards show. The show host, Rob Riggle, stood in the casino, next to Price, showing hockey fans pictures of him in action, and asking them for their thoughts on hockey goalies, his worthiness to be MVP, and other questions.

The fans being interviewed responded with brutal frankness without realizing that they were standing next to the guy they were talking about. Once it was pointed out to them that

Price was standing right there, their shocked reactions were really funny. A lot of expletives had to be bleeped out![6]

The irony of the hockey fans not recognizing Price is that when attending NHL games, there is probably a good chance that they may have given the goalie a standing ovation and cheered his name. As I'm sure you know, hockey goalies wear masks, and so that is how people recognize them. When they take the mask off, they are often anonymous.

My mask for at least half the first thirty years of my life was football player. Sure, I was more than a football player, but if you asked anybody, even me, "Who is Paul McDonald?" the answer would have been, "Oh, he's a quarterback." I first earned my name playing QB at Bishop Amat High, then USC, and finally in the NFL.

While I was playing, I intellectually knew that it wouldn't last forever. But emotionally, I also knew I had to stay completely engaged in my sport to perform at my best. If I started thinking and preparing for my next chapter in life, it would probably arrive too soon. Ultimately, my time to say goodbye to football came in 1988 when I spoke with Tom Landry, the legendary head coach for the Dallas Cowboys. I was called into his office at the end of training camp, and he informed me I was released from the team—and, just like that, my football career was over.

Now what?

The transition from professional sports to the real world (life after sports) is daunting for every athlete that experiences it. I spent most of my entire life preparing for, practicing, and playing football. And then, it's suddenly over. I had a wife and two children with monthly expenses that didn't stop just because football stopped. We had been able to save some money, but the salaries in the '80s were probably around 10 percent of what they are today.

Bottom line, I needed a job and fast!

When I walked into the private banking operation of a major national bank in downtown Los Angeles in the fall of 1988 for my first day of work, there were no bands playing or cheerleaders performing. There was no introduction across the company intercom. No raving fans were asking for an autograph. And there were no media asking for interviews following the day's work.

Just like Price, not wearing his goalie mask, my football mask was put away, and nobody seemed to know or care that just a short while ago, I was flinging footballs in massive stadiums. My new mask was rookie businessman. I might as well have been invisible. In fact, when I walked through the front door, I had to ask someone where my desk was. The first person I encountered showed me an open desk with a phone and said, "Here, this should do." This was the start of my business career. Man, I felt lost!

I know this is the emotional experience of countless athletes, regardless of their sport or how long they played. Whether they were a starter or never saw the field, they all experienced this sense of being out of place, even lost during their transition from sports.

Why?

Nothing in the "real world" really compares to playing a game. So many people love sports, and having the unbelievable good fortune of getting to play at a higher level, whether college or pro, is hard to let go of. It is so rewarding to hone your craft at something that you're really good at and which sets you apart. And the camaraderie of working together with a group of people, who become great friends, to win games and championships, is an amazing thrill that is hard to match.

It was fun! It was fun to compete! It was fun to play a game that we all grew up watching and playing as children. That is really it; the game took us back to our youth. To the time when life was simple, and we just got to play with our friends.

In society today, when you meet someone for the first time, the typical question you hear is "What do you do?" or "Tell me about yourself." The answers typically revolve around your career. We don't hear "Who are you?" which is what's most important. Unfortunately, our identities tend to define us. And, the most prominent identity is typically associated with our profession, our work.

So, due to all the intoxicating positives of being a professional athlete, we have a challenging time accepting "former" in front of athlete. If you are a former athlete, the next question you will receive is generally "What are you doing now?" The answer to this frightening question will most likely not live up to our past life. Imagine meeting your childhood hero, who pitched in the World Series or was the point guard on an Olympic championship basketball team, and they answer, "Oh, I sell copy machines." This is why so many athletes are resistant to the inevitable transition. Their identity has been lost.

Athletes are not the only people who wear masks. The lab coat of a doctor or the thousand-dollar suit of a Hollywood executive can be just as much of a uniform as shoulder pads and a helmet. These clothes tell the world who I am; I am a surgeon or a producer. So many of us wrap our identity around what we do and not who we are.

Others wear a mask to hide.

Go check your social media feed, and you will find numerous pictures of people wearing masks to show off. You can see their groovy lives being played out at trendy restaurants, fun parties, or on exotic vacations. Let's be honest, most of us are guilty at some point of exaggerating the fabulousness of our lives with some well-placed images on Instagram.

Sometimes masks are worn by us as a response to our own deep-rooted issues that we have yet to overcome. However, since we haven't been able to move through these issues, we overcompensate and wear a disguise to project a much more "put together" persona. These masks serve as protective armor for us. They protect us from being real. They protect us from having to be vulnerable. Unfortunately, they also prevent us from being the authentic person we were designed to be, and this holds us back from being truly joyful.

While still playing football, one of my masks was worn to project the image of being the cool, logical, and intellectual quarterback. I hid the fact that I have deep and sensitive emotions. It is embarrassing, but I cry during heartwarming films. Picture that—the NFL quarterback and leader of the offense starts tearing up at a team movie. I imagined that the rash of verbal abuse from my teammates would be brutal, so I held back and just stared stoically at the screen.

Here's the thing. I *imagined* how humiliating it would be to cry in front of my teammates. Yeah, they probably would have teased me, but it would have been lighthearted, and many of them might have privately thought it was cool that I was big-hearted enough to be moved by the story. And for the others, who maybe thought I was a snowflake for crying, so what?

Knowing who you are and what matters to you is a great way of not allowing the opinions of others to concern you. We wear these masks to create illusions and meet the expectations of what we think other people have for us. Don't let the fake coolness of social media or other people's opinions and expectations stop you from being authentic and honest with yourself and others about who you are and what you want.

Easy, right? Maybe not.

After having to transition from football to the business world, I put on a new mask, a businessman. On the drive home, after my first day at my new job, I knew I had no choice. I had a family, and I needed to make money for them. I might not like what I had to do, but I knew I could do it.

The good news for former athletes is they have built a toolkit of life experiences from playing their sport. These learned life skills include how to handle pressure, adjust to change, work with others, keep getting back up when knocked down, dig deep to bring out more than you thought you had in the tank, and so on.

It is an impressive list if we let go of the sports identity and focus on who we are as a person and what we bring to the table learned from an incredibly unique experience as an athlete. I brought all of these qualities to my new profession, which helped me at every step of my business career.

The thing I didn't do was to stop and consider who I really was at the bottom of my being. I just swapped masks from football to business, and it was not until I decided to dig deep to discover the real Paul that I found true joy.

The fact is we all have many identities—father, mother, son, daughter, brother, sister, friend, singer, artist, etc. No matter how many identities we have, they do not define us! We are much more than our identities. It is our qualities as a person that matter most: how we treat people, how we treat ourselves, how we see the world, what has meaning to us, and what we give to others.

WHO DO I WANT
TO BECOME?

THE CHOSEN ONE.

LeBron James was still only a junior in high school when he was featured on the cover of *Sports Illustrated*. The cover headline called LeBron "the chosen one" and named him the heir apparent to NBA legend Michael Jordan.[7] After graduating from high school, LeBron was the number one overall pick in the NBA Draft, and his ensuing spectacular basketball career proved the cover to be prophetic. LeBron excelled so highly at basketball at such a young age that it is hard to believe that football was his first love, and he almost didn't even play organized sports.

LeBron's mother, Gloria, had him when she was sixteen and raised him as a single mom. Although Gloria has been widely credited with being a great mom who poured love into LeBron, the family's dire financial situation caused them to move around a lot and often sleep on the couches of friends in their hometown of Akron, Ohio.[8]

When LeBron was in fourth grade, he was a lonely kid who missed over eighty days of school because he and his mom moved around so much that it became challenging to get to class. During this period, he was spotted by Bruce Kelker, a local youth football coach who was putting together a team and was impressed by his size. LeBron not only had size, but he also had speed, so Kelker made him the team running back. [9]

LeBron was handed the ball on his first-ever play from scrimmage, and he ran eighty yards for a touchdown. Then everything changed. LeBron discovered he was good at sports, and his confidence grew from there. But something else, more important, happened that would impact the rest of his life.

Kelker and his girlfriend invited Gloria and LeBron to move in with them. Gloria became the team mom. A support system, something LeBron previously lacked, was found through sports. He later moved in with the family of Frank Walker. LeBron played on Walker's basketball team, and his son, Frankie Jr., became one of LeBron's friends. [10]

The love, loyalty, and support that LeBron received from his coaches and his community manifested itself into the man that LeBron became. He never forgot it after becoming one of the greatest players in the history of basketball. He has taken great care to share his treasure with the less fortunate in numerous places, but especially for the kids where he grew up in Akron.

LeBron has created a foundation that has provided thousands of students from Akron with full scholarships to attend Akron University. [11] He also never forgot the struggles he faced when in elementary school and created the I Promise School for at-risk kids to give them the stable learning environment he didn't have.[12]

If you asked anyone, LeBron included, what they thought he would become when he was in fourth grade, the answer might have been not much. If you had asked the same question when he was a star hoopster in high school, the easy response would have been an NBA basketball player. LeBron might now be identified as a star basketball player, but the real indication of who he has become can better be measured in the lives he has changed because of his decision to emulate those that helped him and do the same for so many others.

LeBron's decision to share the fruits of his talents to help young people didn't stop him from continuing to pursue his dream to be the best basketball player he could be. You can, and should, strive to be your best self while also taking the time to serve the needs of others.

LeBron's choice to do this undoubtedly made him a better person, but interestingly, it might have made him a better basketball player too. Being an all-star and winning championships grows his earning potential which can be used to help his family, friends, and people in the community. LeBron isn't just playing for himself; he plays to serve others. This sense of purpose provides a powerful role in helping people achieve their goals. It is why teams that play for each other instead of for themselves are the ones that win championships.

As you think about who you want to become, your career is certainly a big part of that equation, but you should also be asking yourself what kind of friend, spouse, parent, and community member you want to be. What are your dreams? How do your dreams impact others? What kind of person do you want to become? You may not yet know the answers to these questions. I didn't. I didn't know until later in life when I consciously shifted as a person and decided who I wanted to be.

After my desert experience, I wanted to have a greater degree of gratitude and peace within me. I wanted to be a more caring, relaxed, and understanding person, someone able to be transparent and connect with others at a deeper level. I wanted to be abundance-minded in all ways concerning personal finances and career. Most of all, as I moved through life, I wanted to be more conscious and pay attention to the messages I would be receiving. Those messages came to me in interesting ways.

I mentioned my propensity to cry during emotional movies. However, I didn't clarify what it exactly was that made me cry. I don't typically cry during sad movies. The inspiring ones when the main character overcomes all odds to achieve their victory have me pulling for the tissue box.

I tear up when I see individuals slowly overcome self-doubt and start to believe as their commitment, determination, and utilization of their unique gifts are used to get over the mountain placed in front of them. Time and time again, these stories resonate with me and bring my hidden emotions to the surface. The thing that inspires me the most is seeing other people reach their full potential.

As I began to see all the positive benefits that my new outlook was having on my life, I slowly began to understand how important it was to me to share my knowledge with others. Writing this book to help others is who I want to become. It is my dream. It is why I am here.

Through my life experiences and the people I've been fortunate to learn from, I can open the door for other people to create their own miracles, thus creating mine. It's an opportunity to provide inspiration to people so they can have their own real empowered moments. What could be better than that?

As you think about who you want to become, dive inward to understand where your real passions reside and how your past experiences have shaped who you are today. Imagine the day after winning a major trophy in sports, business, or life. What would you do next? Who would it be with? What would be the underlying purpose or motivation that drove you to win that trophy?

The answers to these questions make up some of the puzzle pieces of who you want to become. As you start dreaming of the life that you want for yourself, there is a critical principle that will allow you to get there. It is belief.

II. BELIEVE

*Believe you are a miracle and
that change is possible*

ROARING OUT OF
THE TUNNEL

January 1, 1979; The Rose Bowl Players
Tunnel, Pasadena, California

AS I SLOWLY WALKED DOWN the tunnel with my USC
Trojan football teammates, I could feel the adrenaline pulsating around me. We were ready to play. It was the most iconic
game in all of college football, the Rose Bowl, and we were
playing against the Michigan Wolverines. The eyes of the
nation would certainly be glued to the television for the clash
of these two powerhouse teams. There was a lot at stake. We
were ranked third in the country, and Michigan was number
five. National championship possibilities were available to
the winning team.

This is what you sign up for when you play at a school
like USC—the opportunity to come through the tunnel with
everything on the line.

You can see a similar scene in the tunnel before every game of the football season. A team gets pumped up and then roars out the tunnel for the start of the game. I had the amazing opportunity to do that on Sundays with the Cleveland Browns and Dallas Cowboys, but my favorite trips through the tunnel were on Saturdays with my USC teammates. Our roar was special. It was a quiet roar—a confident one.

We believed.

As we moved further down the tunnel and closer to the field, I looked to my right and gave a quiet nod to Ronnie Lott. He would later become one of the best safeties ever to play the game. On my left was Charles White, who would win a Heisman Trophy the following year, crowning him the best player in college football. I also saw other players who were not starters, along with walk-ons, who rarely saw the field. To a man, everyone was locked in. It was not arrogance or machismo; it was a confidence, a belief, a knowing that we were going to win today. The amazing thing is we had this look, this feeling, for every game.

You would think our players would be uptight and nervous as we made our way down the tunnel. I mean, come on, this was a huge match-up. The whole country would be watching us play Michigan in the Rose Bowl with a national championship potentially on the line. It would be easy to let the bright lights of the moment get the best of us. Fear of failure and performance anxiety are commonplace in major athletic competitions, but that level of apprehension did not exist with these Trojan players.

Why such belief? Our players believed in each other because they held each other accountable every single day, and that started with the leaders on the team. If you saw a future NFL player busting his butt every day, you would surely follow, and we had a lot of those guys. We also had incredible coaches, led by College Football Hall of Fame head coach John Robinson and a litany of world-class assistant coaches like iconic defensive line coach Marv Goux and offensive line coach Hudson Houck. Others, like John Jackson, Norv Turner, Bob Toledo, Paul Hackett, and Don Lindsey, all pushed us beyond our limits. The coaches put expectations on themselves and us not only to win but to win it all. It starts with winning the first game, and then the next one, and the next one.

This journey down the tunnel didn't start a few minutes prior as we exited the locker room. It began many months before as we entered the weight room. The preparation for stepping onto the field begins in the offseason—lifting weights, watching film, running, throwing, catching, blocking, and tackling. This is where the path to the tunnel begins. The confidence you get on game day comes from countless hours of practice you put in beforehand to be prepared for the big moments when you are given the opportunity to shine. This isn't just football; it's life. You know you're going to ace that test, or make the sale, or get a great evaluation. You know, because you did the work.

The work we did at USC had an added edge, which fueled our belief. We had the luxury of competing and practicing against each other. This was a huge advantage; a significant part of our team would have a chance to play professionally, and we were as many as three-deep in certain positions. Guys like Brad Budde, Anthony Muñoz, Keith Van Horne, Dennis

Smith, Lynn Cain, Larry McGrew, etc., went on to play a long time in the NFL. It was a ridiculous bounty of riches by college football standards. Iron sharpens iron, so we made each other better even before the season began. It's easy to be the big fish in a small pond, but are you willing to dive into the ocean where the sharks swim? That can be scary, but if you have the courage to test yourself against the best, you will find your skills building and your confidence growing.

To increase your likelihood of success, you must be confident in the things you are attempting to accomplish. But where does this confidence and belief come from when you are starting something for the first time? This sense of belief that you can win starts with the little things, the small successes that build upon one another. First, you have a good summer workout. Then you understand a play design in the classroom, which translates to the practice field, where you execute it perfectly. Next, you have a good session on the field and then a good complete practice that includes an intra-squad scrimmage.

This isn't just the secret to building confidence in becoming a better football player; it is the foundation for any success. It's a simple formula—preparation leads to confidence, and confidence leads to belief. This takes time. As they say, "Rome was not built in a day." Almost everything in life that you can get good at is a step-by-step process. You might not be an expert when trying something new that interests you. But day by day, it becomes more natural, and at some point, you can't even remember the thing that might have once seemed so daunting because it's now second nature. That is how confidence begins to build. As you have more positive experiences in practice, your self-belief also continues to grow when the bright lights are on.

In the game, all the work you have done allows you the freedom of just letting it rip and play with confidence because you have already done it hundreds of times before. They say practice like you play and play like you practice. This is 100 percent correct, and it is where confidence and self-belief come from.

As we approached the end of the tunnel and you could hear the roar of the USC fans at the Rose Bowl, excited to see our team perform—excited to see the Trojans win again, especially against the powerful Michigan Wolverines. The crazy thing is that almost every USC supporter and fan in the stands also believed we would win this day! Positive energy surrounded the entire Trojan half of the Rose Bowl, which all emanated from the players, coaches, staff, and the belief we had developed long before we moved through the tunnel!

Oh, and the game? We won 17–10 and were crowned national champions in the coaches poll.

The belief was real.

HALF-EMPTY OR HALF-FULL?

THIRTEEN YEARS AFTER I FINISHED playing at USC, the belief that my teammates and I had in the tunnel was pretty much gone. USC had not won any national championships since our 1978 season, and Trojan fans were not happy.

Trojan supporters and fans were openly critical that the team was no longer competing for national championships. USC head coach Larry Smith responded by saying that you don't win games because of the logo on your helmet. In other words, the tradition of being a powerhouse football program didn't count for much when the team stepped onto the field. Smith would later add in an interview with the *LA Times*, "College football is not the way it was 20 years or 30 years ago. Far too many people, alumni and administrators, think everything can continue to be like it was 20 years ago. It can't. I think they're hung up on what happened in the '60s and '70s. I don't think anything will change."[13]

Coach Smith was essentially saying that USC could not have that same expectation of victory that my generation of Trojans had when we entered the tunnel. And for the next eight years, the 1993–2000 seasons, those words rang prophetic as USC went 58–39–2. Respectable for some programs, but nowhere near the national championship level of play that Trojan fans expected from their team. In that period, there was only one Rose Bowl win, and the team did not even qualify for a bowl game in four of the eight seasons—unheard of for USC football. Even the Trojan faithful began to question whether a return to greatness was possible.

And then, in the ninth year, it seemed to get even worse. In its search for a new football coach, USC kept getting turned down by the candidates it was recruiting. They finally hired a guy named Pete Carroll, who had a lifetime NFL head coaching record of 34–33 and had just been fired by the New England Patriots the previous year. Honestly, hiring Pete didn't inspire much hope among the fans who immediately (and loudly) voiced their disapproval.

By that 2001 season, when Coach Carroll got started, I was in my fourth year as the color analyst for USC football radio broadcasts, and I was in the press box on October 13 for a Trojans game versus Arizona State. USC had started the season 1–4, and the announced attendance on that day was only 43,508. When you consider that the Coliseum had over ninety-thousand seats for football games, you could surmise that the stadium was either half-full or half-empty. I think it would be safe to say that Trojan fans saw the coliseum as half-empty. The vast majority of people filing into the stadium on that day didn't have the same expectations of victory that my teammates and I had when we came running out the tunnel during our games in the late 1970s.

I think it is quite possible that most coaches running out onto the field for that game would have begun to lose confidence and be in fear for their jobs, but Pete had already been fired many times before, so what was there to lose? He had learned that you would inevitably have failures in your life. So, instead of being paralyzed by fear, the best response to adversity (really the only response) is to trust and believe in yourself, your teammates, and your program. To give it all you've got, have fun, and don't let yourself get emotionally married to what the outcome might be.

In the year after the Patriots fired him, Pete went on a self-imposed hiatus from football where he spent the time diving inward to rethink what his philosophies would be the next time he got the opportunity to coach a football team.

One of the biggest epiphanies Pete brought with him to USC was to be authentic. He wasn't going to coach like anybody else. He wasn't going to be like anyone else. He was going to be Pete; his team would also be unique and true to themselves. Consequently, the culture he created was fiercely competitive; the practices were often more challenging than the games.

Pete also made practice and the games fun! Fans were lined up five deep at practice and at the games to watch the high-octane head coach, assistant coaches, and players perform and entertain. Everyone ran around the field with a sense of urgency to get better and to be the best. Pete was insanely positive and upbeat and created an environment that focused on instilling self-confidence instead of using fear of failure as the motivating force for the players.

It is impossible to play freely if you are afraid that the outcome will be negative. In an interview with *The Seattle Times*, Pete drew an analogy to explain how doing the preparation and then playing freely with confidence nets the best results. He said, "Think of a dancer. Dancers work and they work and they work and they master their skill—or singers—they master their skills so far that improvisation just comes flowing out of them. Their natural expression of the best they can possibly be comes out of them because there is no boundary to hold them back."[14]

On October 13, 2001, in front of a half-full coliseum, the USC football team started to dance! They defeated Arizona State 38–17. The team would go on to win four of its next five games before losing in the Las Vegas Bowl to finish 6–6. It did not seem like much, but you don't have to be a diehard college football fan to know what happened next at USC.

At the conclusion of the 2002 season, the Trojans were invited to the Orange Bowl, where they easily defeated the Iowa Hawkeyes 38–17. The team finished 11–2 and was ranked number four in the nation. The next season USC finished 12–1 with a Rose Bowl victory over Michigan to capture the national title—the first championship since 1978 when the Trojans won it during my junior year at the university. Winning the Orange Bowl and then the national title, with Pete Carroll at the helm, marked the start of a golden era of Trojan football.

The belief had returned.

DO I BELIEVE?

IF YOU'RE A SPORTS FAN, you have watched this scene numerous times over the years. The final seconds tick off the game clock, it hits zero, and the players and coaches on one of the sidelines start to jump around, hugging each other. They have just won a championship.

Within seconds of shaking hands with the vanquished opponent, the winning team's star quarterback, point guard, or shortstop is being interviewed on TV by the sideline reporter. The player inevitably says the reason that he and his teammates are champions is that they never lost belief in their ability to win it all, even when so many others doubted them.

Most of us know that in order to win championships, really, to be successful at anything, it is important to have self-belief. This is true for individuals, teams, or for any group of people in an organization. Self-belief is often the difference between the woman who makes the all-star team and the one who has some talent but sits on the bench, rarely getting any playing time—or the wide salary gap between the top salesman in a company and the one struggling just to make his numbers.

But what about the team that lost the championship game? Did they lose their belief with that loss? It's easy to believe when you're winning, but what about when you're losing?

Here's the thing; you're not going to win every game. Even the great Trojan teams that won thirty-four games consecutively during the 2003–2005 seasons lost to an outstanding Texas squad, led by Vince Young in the '06 championship game. If there are thirty-two teams in a league, there is only one champion. Does that make the players on the other thirty-one teams losers? If your belief in yourself or your team is built completely on winning, does it go away when you lose a game, or worse yet, many games? True belief is not only believing in yourself when you are on a winning streak; it is keeping your belief when all others have seemingly given up hope.

Your self-belief can't only be validated by the trophies you win or by others telling you how great you are. It has to come from within. People with true self-belief don't waver when they are defeated; they choose to learn from their failures so that they can grow and get better. A common trait of champions is their ability to acknowledge that they fell short of their goals, but then they get up, get stronger, and continue working to be the best they can be.

We are all inspired by stories of underdogs that climb out of the gutter and overcome all odds to become champions somehow. It is why so many people consider *Rocky* to be their all-time favorite movie. Many of us might see ourselves in the guy from the wrong side of the tracks, who has had nothing but a series of disappointments in his life, only to finally get his shot and rise to the occasion. It makes us feel good because it gives us hope and makes us believe that we can one day achieve greatness, if only for a moment.

If we are perfectly honest with ourselves, the warm glow of inspiration that we feel from other people's Rocky moments quickly fades, and we soon slide back into the comfortable numbness of our daily lives. We believe that great things can happen, but just not for us.

I'm here to tell you that great things are possible. Greatness is not just for others but is something that you can achieve. We all have amazing gifts within us to share with the world. Miracles can happen, and all miracles start with the belief that our unique set of gifts can be used to make the world a better place. Read that again. Miracles happen when we start to believe our own set of gifts can make the world a better place.

Yes, my Trojan teammates and I walked through the tunnel believing we would win—and we almost always did. But the best kind of belief comes with knowing that we get to stand on the shoulders of those victories and use them to do something that helps others. As you go through your personal tunnel, belief will play a massive role in determining the life you live. Having purpose attached to the belief leads to the joy we all seek when entering the arena.

However, even if in your heart of hearts you want to do right by your family, community, the world, you might still struggle with believing in yourself. This can especially be true when consequences of life put you in a position to doubt that you will ever get over the hump and start living a better life. Do not despair. Self-belief can be learned, it can be practiced, and it can lead you to live your own Rocky moments.

CHANGE IS POSSIBLE

THE INABILITY TO SEE THINGS for how they could be as opposed to how they are is a limitation that many people possess. Larry Smith didn't see a future where national champions were possible. But when Pete Carroll took over as coach, he could imagine a return to national prominence—even after starting his first season 1–4. That imagination became a reality. A year after finishing 6–6, Carroll's Trojans were Orange Bowl champions, and a year later, USC defeated Michigan in the Rose Bowl, and the team was voted the AP National Champions. The mindset at USC had changed from having limited dreams to one where there were no limits. However, for some people, the need for change is more dire than winning or losing some football games. Caron Butler is a perfect example.

Butler was just twelve years old when he began selling drugs on the street. By the time he was fifteen years old, he had already been arrested fifteen times, but if anyone can be held up as an example that change is possible, it is Butler. He was able to catapult from that cold reality of selling drugs on the street and prison to a lucrative fourteen-year career in the NBA, where he made the All-Rookie team and twice appeared in the All-Star game.[15]

Butler grew up in a rough neighborhood in Racine, Wisconsin, where the temptation to make easy money selling drugs was more than he could avoid. He joined a gang and started selling drugs in a park that was nearby his house. Butler soon took possession of a handgun to protect himself against rival gangs, and he was in several shootouts during his middle school years.

An exceptional basketball player, Butler would divide his time between selling drugs, playing hoops, and going to school. However, that all changed when his last arrest resulted in him being sentenced to two years in prison. At the age of fifteen, when most kids were just getting acclimated to life in high school, Butler would be spending his time in a cell at the Ethan Allan School, a correctional facility for boys.[16]

The path that Butler chose necessitated change. The outcome for young people who join a gang, sell drugs, and carry a gun is inevitably prison or death. Even with those two extremely negative options staring them in the face, many people don't make the changes necessary to save their life because they don't think change is possible. They can't imagine it.

In his autobiographical book, *Tuff Juice*, Butler acknowledged that even going to prison didn't alter his course. When he first arrived at the juvenile jail, his mindset was the same as most other prisoners—become a smarter drug dealer who took the proper steps to not get caught the next time he was on the street. His cellmates even counseled him on how to conduct himself as a criminal after he was released—ways to avoid getting caught by the police and how to always stay one step ahead of them.[17]

While at the correctional facility, Butler got into a fight with another prisoner, which landed him in solitary confinement—a place they called "The Hole." Being sent to prison didn't snap Butler out of his criminal mindset, but The Hole was such a terrible experience that he finally vowed to change. Butler wrote in the book that no matter how high the mountain, he would do everything in his power to navigate through life's challenges in an honest way, and a lifestyle that would land him back in prison was not an option.

After Butler was released and back home in Racine, his resolve was challenged when his peers would mock him for his minimum wage job at Burger King while they rolled in the big bucks peddling drugs. Although he didn't have an easy path to a better life, Butler's decision to change was unwavering. He made the decision to change, and that change took him from the lowest of the lows of solitary in prison to the highest of the highs playing basketball in the NBA.[18]

Unfortunately, for many people, the decision to change only comes after they hit rock bottom. For Butler, rock bottom was spending two weeks of solitary confinement in prison. For others, it might be a health scare, like a heart attack, a bankruptcy, the threat of divorce from their spouse, or a death in the family.

The flipside for many people is that they never really hit rock bottom but walk through life in a trance, a never-ending rut that they can't seem to get out of. They are stuck for so long that change seems impossible, and the desire to want more from life has long gone. They work at a job they hate, selling products they don't believe in, for a boss they don't like. But they never leave.

They never leave unless they wake up because the fear of the unknown is immensely more powerful than the malaise and unhappiness resulting from living an unfulfilled life. So, even though their life sucks, at least they know what to expect. If they change, their life could be worse.

We get one life, and we owe ourselves so much more than living it like a zombie where a six-pack and a ball game on TV serve as the antidote for a life not lived. You can wait for a terrible rock bottom moment to snap you out of your trance, or you can avoid the pain of that crisis by simply deciding that the time has arrived to climb out of the rut.

I decided in 2010 that it was time to climb out of my rut when I chose to figure things out in Indian Wells. I wasn't in prison, going through a divorce, or in a hospital with a rare disease. I had wandered off my path, and I decided enough was enough. It was time to create a new path for me.

I am here to tell you that change is possible. If a fifteen-year-old kid can decide to humble himself in front of his peers by taking a low-level job at Burger King as a simple first step to getting his life on track, then you can do the necessary things to get yours going too.

Miracles can happen. Caron Butler switched from a path that included gangs and prison to one that led to a stellar NBA career. You might not have the goals or the ability to achieve the status of a professional athlete, but that does not mean you cannot live a life of joy that is equal to or even greater than the players you watch on TV. We all deserve to live a life of joy.

Although Caron made some poor choices at a young age that resulted in prison time, he didn't let those decisions define him for the rest of his life. In his heart, he knew that he was better than the tough guy role he played on the street. When he decided to be real with who he was and who he wanted to be and stopped playing the role of what others expected him to be, that's when it all changed, and life opened up for him.

III. BE AUTHENTIC

*Strive to be your best authentic self,
not someone else's version*

EXPECTATIONS
OF OTHERS

THE EXPECTATIONS OTHERS have of you are a heavy burden to carry. Your friends at school don't like it when you act in a way outside the social norm for the campus. Your parents have very clear ideas on what your major should be in college. Your spouse wants to be supportive but is nervous about your idea to give up your safe job in exchange for chasing your dream career.

It is often the case that people's expectations of you match their own insecurities and the limited expectations they have for themselves. Many people tend to squash the dreams of others because they can't imagine achieving their own dreams. I don't believe that most people who do this are being petty or mean. They honestly can't believe that it is possible to see dreams come true.

I always wanted to play quarterback at a major university, especially for one of those football teams that were able to compete in New Year's Day bowl games. It was my dream. That dream could have been shattered when it was my leg that got shattered during the last regular-season game of my junior year at Bishop Amat High School.

I broke my leg in three places and had a long road to recovery, which stretched well into my senior season. I was a lightly recruited quarterback with no national championship-caliber schools offering me a scholarship to play quarterback—except for the University of Southern California.

Wow!

I grew up watching the Trojans play. Many kids from my generation in Southern California rooted for USC football in the fall and UCLA basketball in the winter because those were the two national powerhouse programs on the West Coast at the time. I was a football guy, so it was all USC for me, even though I was recruited by the Bruins for a short period. In addition, when I was in middle school, the Trojans quarterback was Pat Haden, which was especially cool for me because Pat also played quarterback at my high school, Bishop Amat.

Going to USC was an easy choice, but after it was announced that I would be attending on a football scholarship, the star player on our high school basketball team began quizzing me. Why USC? I was honestly taken aback at first. Well, the Trojans seemed to be in the Rose Bowl almost every year, competed for national championships, and assuming I would be living in Southern California, there was no better school from which to get my college degree.

The star player was obviously aware of all that, but he was just as puzzled at my decision to pick USC as I was at his questioning of my choice. He mentioned to me that he knew I had also received scholarship offers to play at other smaller schools and one "middle of the pack" school in the Pac-12 conference (back then the Pac-10).

And then he came out with it: "Don't you want to play?" He believed that if I joined one of the smaller or less successful programs, I would have a better chance to play than if I went to SC, where I would be destined to a career of sitting on the bench. I politely smiled (I don't think he saw that I was gritting my teeth) and repeated to him that choosing to be a Trojan was a no-brainer for me. To myself, I was saying, "We'll see." Not that I needed it, but this conversation provided just a bit more motivation as I arrived on campus.

Imagine a world where you get to set your own expectations, grand and small—where you live on your own terms. Where you get to create the life you want! So, what's holding you back from living the life you desire, one that is authentic to you and not the one that others expect from you?

I was intuitive enough that I didn't let my classmate's insecurities become my own. I didn't allow his limited expectations to become how I set expectations for myself. Not everyone is as fortunate. Many people, especially the young, haven't developed the confidence to stand apart from the pack and choose a path that is right for them.

Peer pressure can play a major role in setting expectations that are not authentic to us.

An inner-city school principal once told me the story of creating a rule that the entire student body had to take all their books home every day. Why? It was to give cover to the kids who did want to study but didn't want to be considered uncool for being "book nerds." He was combating the negative peer pressure that can often be found in high schools. Many students have not yet found the strength and confidence to live an authentic life.

Bending to the expectations of others and not living an authentic life is a sad reality for lots of people. They follow a path laid out for them instead of paving a path designed by them. They live the life they feel they're supposed to live— that of a dutiful child or someone just trying to fit in. Do not misunderstand me; we should listen to our parents and mentors about directions in life. A vast majority of parents have years of wisdom to tap into, and they want what is best for us, so their opinion should be given great weight. However, when placing expectations on others, even when they are well-meaning, some people fall into traps that lead to giving or accepting poor advice.

Parents, spouses, and friends, you should ask yourself some important, honest, and yes, tough questions when you provide advice to your loved ones. Is the advice you are offering something that you think they *should* be doing, even if it doesn't fit their aptitude or personality? Are you asking them to reach goals beyond their capacity, or conversely, are you settling for limits because you fear they will be hurt if they fail?

Parents, are you hoping your children will achieve a certain status because it will make you feel good about yourself? As an example, many people dream of high-status professions for their kids, but whose dream is it? A parent may want their child to be a doctor or lawyer because those are reputable, honorable careers. Many children follow this path chosen for them and end up miserable.

Unfortunately, these hopes for our children often overcome us when we let our ego become too attached to their achievements and status. The college cheating scandal of 2019, where people paid bribes and lied to get their kids into top universities, is a good example of this. Every student has their own path, and they should be encouraged and supported to become the very best person that they can be and not try to be what society sets as the gold standard.

Deep down, we all know what is right for us. There is no need to fall in line with the norm! There is no need to line up to please others to earn their approval just to fit in. This is especially challenging during the formative years of our youth when we are searching for our tribe, our posse, and our own identity.

Know that it says a lot about who you are by what school you attend, what career you are in, or what friends you hang out with. But these things don't define you! And, they certainly don't define who you want to become. Our answers to what we want, how we feel, or who we are do not reside in our personas, our identities. They don't reside within other people's opinions of us either.

All the answers we are searching for reside within us. We just need to be honest with ourselves and others.

TRUE CONFIDENCE

IT WAS LATE IN THE SEASON of my senior year at Bishop Amat High when we lined up against the Servite Friars for a huge game that would set the tone for the upcoming playoffs. If we won, we would make the playoffs with a good seed. A loss meant limping into the postseason without much confidence. I stood under center with about a minute left in the game. It was fourth down and four yards to go, and we were knocking on the door, just fifteen yards from the end zone.

You've heard this story before—game on the line, and the quarterback throws the winning touchdown pass to save the day. The crowd rushes the field, and he is carried off the field on the shoulders of his teammates. That's what I had always envisioned. Pretty cool, huh?

Well, it didn't quite happen that way. In fact, it could not have been worse!

I surveyed the field quickly because I told the team in the huddle that the snap would be on the first sound to catch the defense by surprise. As I placed my hands under center, I knew something wasn't right, but I couldn't wait because my guys were going to take off on my first command. So, I said, "Hut," and the offensive line fired off the line of scrimmage. The ball never touched my hands. It went straight up into the air resulting in a fumble that we didn't recover. It was a surreal moment that I was trying to process. I was thinking, "What just happened!?"

A moment or two after the chaos of the scrum for the ball occurred, I realized what had happened. I hadn't lined up under center; I got behind the guard! It's a total boneheaded mistake. And it was embarrassing beyond belief, to say the least. It was all my fault! Not only did we lose the game, but I was the laughingstock on campus that night and the days that followed.

The night after the debacle, I received a call from Paul Hackett. At the time, he was the University of California's quarterback coach and was at the game scouting for recruits. I was sheepish in responding to his praise of my play in the game. And then he said, "I had to leave the game early and catch a flight and, as I was going, I heard some commotion on the field. What happened?"

Remember, Hackett was recruiting me to play at a great school, where I would have a good chance to play for two to three years. And, it was free—a full-ride scholarship! I didn't want to do anything to screw up that opportunity. If he had already left, could I find a way to sidestep the question? I mean, how would he respond? Who wants to be the guy recruiting a quarterback that lines up under guard for one of the biggest plays of the season?

On the other hand, I was still confident in my abilities as a player and felt that if this put him in the position of needing to look elsewhere for a quarterback, I could find somewhere to play, even if it is wasn't at the University of California. This was all going through my mind while I was getting ready to respond. I stammered and said, "Well, you're not going to believe this, but I lined up behind the guard, and we fumbled." Wow! Did I really say that!? Will I ever hear from him again? These thoughts and more were racing through my mind.

Paul Hackett's response was, "Well, that's happened before." This was when I knew he was my guy and that I was following him wherever he coached. About a month later, "Hack" answered new USC head coach John Robinson's call to come to USC to coach quarterbacks. And the rest is history.

When confronted about a mistake you've made, come clean. We're all human and screw up once in a while. The truth will eventually come out, and it's not typically the errors people make that are their downfall. It's the lies they tell to cover them up that bring them down—even presidents (just ask Nixon and Clinton). It takes true confidence to admit you were wrong, that you made a mistake. But, the result of doing so can lead to a life of integrity, fulfillment, and love.

In the classic self-help book by Don Miguel Ruiz, *The Four Agreements*, the first agreement which will lead you on a path towards happiness, joy, and an overall state of well-being is to be impeccable with your word. This agreement focuses on the significance of speaking with integrity and carefully choosing words before saying them aloud. It takes great courage and belief in oneself to admit you are wrong. It takes true confidence.[19]

We are not perfect, so let's all just get over it. Our parents made mistakes when they parented us as children. They still do. Our bosses made mistakes when they managed us. They still do. We all made mistakes as children, parents, athletes, employees, and employers. This will continue as long as we are alive. It's okay.

It's okay as long as we pay attention, learn from our mistakes, and move through them, so they are less likely to happen again. By the way, I played another twelve years of football in college and the NFL, and that was the only time I lined up under the guard. I learned from my mistake.

I never spoke to Paul Hackett about this conversation until forty-five years later. I asked him, "Did you know?"

"I did know," he said. Was he testing me at the time, seeing if I had the fortitude to come clean with a massive mistake that affected my entire team? He was.

The result of my openness and honesty with him that night led us to an uncommon bond between coach and player, a national championship at USC in 1978, and four great years together in the NFL. Most importantly, we remain very close friends to this day. The simple act of having the confidence to tell the truth opened a door for me that I will always cherish and appreciate.

BE YOUR BEST SELF

ARRIVING ON CAMPUS AT USC as a freshman was a dream. I could not stop pinching myself. I was really here! Here was my chance to finally prove all the doubters wrong and the opportunity to play quarterback for a team that was a regular New Year's Day fixture in Pasadena for the Rose Bowl and was in the hunt for a national championship almost every season.

It didn't take long for me to be brought back down to earth.

The first thing that happened was I walked out onto the field for our opening practice and counted eight other quarterbacks. When they all paired up to play catch, I had to grab a student manager to throw with me. As the rookie on the squad, I was on the bottom rung of the totem pole, the ninth string quarterback on a team with nine quarterbacks!

You can't get any lower.

I recalled what my high school classmate tried to warn me about. If you go to a major program like USC, there is a good chance you will be sitting on the bench for four years, a spectator like everyone else in the stadium. I quickly pushed that thought out of my mind and reminded myself that I was here to get better each day with the vision and intention of playing. Ninth was just my starting position. I could do this.

And then I saw Vince Evans.

We were walking down this path that led to the practice field, and I saw someone with no t-shirt on, throwing a football. Seemingly without much effort, each ball the guy threw ripped through the air, traveling as much as seventy yards down field. This dude was built like Adonis. I asked out loud, "Who's the linebacker who can throw the ball like that?"

The wide receiver walking with me said, "No dummy, that's the quarterback. That's Vince Evans."

"Oh my god. If you've got to look like that and throw like that, I will never play here."

Vince Evans could throw the ball a mile. My arm strength was adequate. Vince Evans was lightning fast. I wasn't slow, but there was no comparison to his speed. Vince Evans was big and strong. When I was getting weighed in, Marv Goux, the legendary Trojan assistant coach, yelled out at me, "Hey McDonald, 'What prisoner of war camp did you just get out of?'" My new quarterback coach, Paul Hackett, was a little bit kinder. He just called me "Slim."

I was clearly not Vince Evans.

The problem with much of modern society is that many people want to be someone they cannot become. We all get bombarded with images of a life that seems better than our own, and we feel the need to achieve a high level of status based on other people's gifts and other people's dreams. If the next-door neighbor has a new luxury item—or the kid in class just got into a prestigious university—then it must be something that I should have too. Right?

Trying to be someone else's version of the best can point people in all kinds of directions, none of which will lead to joy and a path of reaching their personal potential.

There are people who believe that their best self can only be satisfied with the accumulation of things that they've seen in glossy magazines. Designer clothing. A luxury car. Fancy jewelry. A big house, yacht, private jet, the list goes on and on. They spend their lives furiously working harder and harder so that they can buy more and more things. On the outside, some of these people have lives that look bright and shiny, but on the inside, things are dark and rotten. The chase is never-ending.

And then there are those who will never accumulate much wealth, but they satisfy those wants by living vicariously through other people's lives. There are numerous global media companies designed to give the audience an escape from the numbness of their own lives by providing them a daily diet of fluff, gossip, and cheap drama. This has always been the case. Stand in line at the supermarket checkout counter, and you will see numerous gossip tabloids that were available for your parents, and even your grandparents, to read.

Where our parents read the National Enquirer, we now watch TMZ, or any number of reality shows, to feed our need for other people's drama. If the news is juicy enough, it might even go viral, which leads us to the latest, and probably most dangerous, way to consume content—social media.

It's easy to beat up on social media and to oversimplify it as a purely negative thing. It's interesting because studies have shown that inspirational content or content that speaks to our goals to make society a better place is actually consumed more often than negative content. Social media has a great place in our society to allow us to connect with each other and share our own personal news like never before. That half of the social media equation is awesome.

However, social media gets dangerous when we start to use it as a means toward creating an illusion of a life that seems great but does not authentically capture who we really are. There is our real life and our Instagram life, and most of us have to admit that the two rarely match.

The massive impact that social media has made in the daily lives of so many people, especially the young, has quite often created a burning need to stand out and prove to the world how perfect our lives are. We are constantly comparing ourselves to others, which we can't help but notice because notifications from our "friends" show up just about every moment on our smartphones.

We post pictures of our exotic vacations or life events and watch to see how many likes we receive from our followers. And, we see similar photos or comments posted from "friends," and we unconsciously compare their coolness factor to ours. This feeling we have, whether it's one of superiority or inferiority to others, is all about our ego.

Eckhart Tolle, in his book *A New Earth, Awakening to Your Life Purpose*, talked about how the hidden motivating force behind ego is generally one or more of the following: "The need to stand out, be special, be in control; the need for power, for attention, for more."[20] He also talked about the ego's need for opposition or enemies. Many of us do this by comparing ourselves to others. If I have more social media "likes" than my "friend," then I must be better and worth more, maybe even deserving of love.

There is no need to be anyone else but *you*! Of the almost eight billion people on this planet, there is *only one you*! There is nobody uniquely like you, so why are we comparing ourselves to each other? There is no need. Instead, our purpose in life should be to grow and evolve each moment of every day. Stop comparing and simply be your best self—not somebody else's, just yours.

I clearly was not Vince Evans, but I still had my dreams. What should I do? The answer was simple. Be the best Paul McDonald that I could be and don't try to be Vince Evans.

I had to get to work.

FOCUS ON YOUR STRENGTHS

AFTER I GOT OVER THE SHOCK of seeing how athletic and strong Vince Evans was, I made a choice. I decided to go to work. Did I go to work to remold myself into the image of Vince? Of course not. I focused on my own gifts.

I was a good student, so I made it my mission to know the playbook better than any quarterback on our team. I also spent countless hours in the film room with the coaches to learn our plays and what other teams' defenses would be throwing at us.

It paid off. On the first day of training camp, I scored the highest among all the quarterbacks when we were tested for our knowledge of the playbook. I might have started ninth on the quarterback depth chart, but I rose to first in that category.

The casual sports fan might think, "Well, McDonald has the brains to be a coach, but just knowing the playbook and studying film won't mean squat when a massive defensive lineman or linebacker is bearing down on him during a game."

It is true that quarterbacks who are faster can use their legs to elude an oncoming defender better.

However, the difference in speed between someone considered fast on the football field and an average runner is only a couple tenths of a second. A cerebral quarterback, who knows the plays, and has relentlessly studied opposing teams' defensive tendencies in the film room, can more than make that time up by recognizing a play on the field as it is unfolding.

To know where the receiver is going and which one will be open is key, but the ability to see it and anticipate the throw before he's open is what sets apart the best from the mediocre. While quarterbacks who don't have this aptitude are still trying to figure out the situation, other ones with this gift already have the ball out of their hand and on the way to the receiver.

The other thing that I had going for me was my throwing accuracy. I was pretty good at pinpointing my passes, and so I worked and worked at getting better. I was constantly refining my footwork and my throwing mechanics until it all became automatic. I practiced these things until it was something I didn't have to think about.

I also let myself be coached. I was a sponge for everything my coaches taught. I didn't have to be spectacular. I just had to be consistently good, and specifically, perform the way Paul Hackett wanted me to. His pet peeve was making poor decisions. So, I had to be smart with the ball in my hands—throwing to the correct receiver, throwing it away when everyone was covered, or even taking a sack, if necessary. And, for God's sake, do not ever throw an interception!

I performed these tasks well because I listened to what was expected of the position. I didn't have the arm strength to throw it through a defender, so I didn't try. I simply got it to the open receiver most of the time. I focused on my strengths and continued to do the work to strive to get better.

I found my way, and the coaches were paying attention to how much I worked. It showed them how badly I wanted the job. That meant a lot during my progression toward becoming USC's starting quarterback a couple of years later.

We are all born with certain specific gifts. Yes, everyone! And, these are gifts that no other person possesses quite like you. The first step is to understand what makes you special. It will generally require a deep dive and might be prompted by reading a book on the subject or speaking to those people who know you intimately. Also, you may work on determining your strengths by journaling or taking a walk at a peaceful location. During this quiet time of reflection, ask yourself a few simple questions.

What do you like doing? What comes easy for you to do or learn? If you were asked to teach something to a beginner, what would be some of the best things you could teach? If you are in a group, what skills or personality attributes can you best contribute to the team's efforts? Do you like engaging with lots of people or prefer working quietly by yourself?

As you read, learn, and reflect on these questions (and many others), you will probably start to recognize qualities that are the easiest and most natural for you to perform. These are the things you should be doing in your life the vast majority of the time.

Why?

If you were engaged with something that comes easiest for you, you will most likely be good at it. In addition, because you are good at it, you will receive positive feedback from others, creating good feelings resulting in a fun experience. It will feel good, which encourages you to do it again and again, and you get better and better. Keep doubling down on your strengths, and this positive cycle will continue to evolve.

If we match our strengths and gifts with our passion in life, then miracles happen!

Miracles will happen when we unleash the power of our unique set of gifts onto the things in life that match our passions. However, an honest assessment of our ability to be successful in our chosen pursuits will require that we also acknowledge that we can't be good at everything and must also be prepared to shore up our weaknesses.

So, what did I need to do to shore up my weaknesses?

Let's start with throwing the long ball. I did not have the powerful arm that could launch the ball sixty- to sixty-five yards downfield on a "go" route, so I would adjust my footwork when dropping back. This was especially important when throwing to the fastest man on the field wearing cardinal and gold, wide receiver Kevin Williams, "the Bug."

Kevin was a sprinter from San Fernando High, the same school that produced Heisman Trophy winner Charles White and defensive back Kenny Moore. His forty-yard dash time was always 4.4 seconds, which back in the '70s, and even today, was lightning fast. So, for me to hit the Bug in stride and put the appropriate loft on the ball, I needed to quicken and slightly shorten my drop back to get the ball out of my hand faster. It was one more thing for me to think about when that play was called, but when I adjusted my feet, I was able to make the throw.

I wasn't known for my speed either. In fact, it was so bad that head coach John Robinson had me work out with the assistant track coach at USC during the offseason. I had several sessions with him, working on my stride and relaxing my body while running. After the third session, he said to me, "You're fast enough; you just have to believe you are." I remember responding, "Really?" I thought he was joking. Obviously, my belief in my speed needed a little work.

Although I found it hard to believe at first, what the track coach told me gave me confidence. I was timed running a forty-yard dash during spring practice leading into my sophomore year and ran the fastest time ever—4.8 seconds—which was outstanding for me. With my newfound belief, I had a few key scrambles versus Alabama and LSU that kept drives alive when I became the starter. So, I guess you could say those sessions to shore up a deficit paid off.

Although working on speed and adjusting my footwork were required, it was not those things that catapulted me from a ninth-string freshman to a senior year All-American. My gifts in understanding the playbook and game film better than anybody and focusing on my accuracy as a passer helped me to stand out.

If I had just worked on my weaknesses, I would never have risen to the caliber of player I became, and I don't think I would have ever gotten off the bench at USC. And that approach—focusing so intently on weaknesses—is a major deficit that our education system currently suffers.

I understand the issues in working with millions of kids and attempting to keep everyone in the center lane of standardization, an attempt to give everyone an acceptable level of competence in all things. However, most people generally have a specific orientation. Either they are good in math or language, for example. If someone is naturally gifted in math, they should spend most of their time on math, not the other way around. You create engineers and scientists by focusing those with math talents on math! You create screenwriters and authors from those gifted in language, so spend more time on literature!

If you play sports, don't force a square peg in a round hole. A three-hundred-pound offensive lineman in American football probably shouldn't play quarterback. But he could be a powerlifter in the Olympics. You can crossover to other sports as long as the same gifts you possess translate to that sport and/or the position you will be playing. For instance, John McEnroe was a very good soccer player in his youth before he began his Hall of Fame tennis career. The soccer skills translated in the form of excellent footwork, which is a requirement for great tennis.

With that said, the scientist still must be able to read, the lineman must still be able to move, and the author must also be able to balance a checkbook. So, spend enough time on those weaker areas to learn the basics that apply to your position in sports or job in life. I was never going to run in the Olympics, but I needed to be just fast enough not to get killed when I dropped back in the pocket!

An obsessive focus on your weaknesses can also carry the danger of creating a negative mindset where you start to doubt your ability to achieve anything in life. How can you think about the good things you can accomplish if you only pay attention to the stuff you are bad at? At its worst, this negative mindset can often prevent people from trying. They are defeated before they even begin.

If you've had a series of negative things that have happened in your life, begin to focus on the positive, the skills that you excel at, and where your passions lie, and you will start to move out of your slump. Rather than allowing your weaknesses to paralyze you, think about the unique strengths that you possess, take a deep breath, and just let it rip. You might be surprised at the outcome.

IV. GO FOR IT!

*Take action and have trust
in the flow of life*

DON'T ASK,
DON'T GET

VINCE PAPALE LOVES SPORTS.

As a senior at Interboro High School, located in suburban Philadelphia, Papale lettered in three sports: football, basketball, and track. Although his greatest love was football (a rabid Eagles fan), his lack of size prevented him from getting any offers to play college ball. However, his speed did earn him a track scholarship at St. Joseph's University in Philadelphia.[21]

After graduating from St. Joe's, Papale returned to Interboro to teach and coach. Still, he never lost his love of football and played in numerous leagues, including for a team sponsored by a local watering hole, Max's Bar. During a hiatus from full-time teaching, while working as a bartender and nightclub doorman, Papale learned about an open tryout that Philadelphia Eagles head coach Dick Vermeil was holding for the team.[22]

This was too good to be true. Papale had been an Eagles ticket holder for ten years, and this tryout would give him the opportunity to go from the stands to the playing field. However, the odds of him making the team were slimmer than slim.[23] What was he up against?

Size: Papale was told in high school that he was too small to play football, and this was the NFL.

Age: Papale was thirty years old. No NFL player, other than a kicker, had ever started their rookie season in their thirties. Ever.

Sheer Numbers: During the era that Papale was trying out, many teams brought 120 players to training camp, which was cut down to a forty-five-man roster. These 120 players pretty much all played college football, many for powerhouse universities such as USC, Notre Dame, and Texas. Papale didn't play college football, and this was a tryout before training camp even started.

If you have seen the movie *Invincible* you know where this story lands. With speed to burn and grit to match, Papale defied all odds to make the team and was later voted special teams captain by his teammates. Honestly, Papale had almost no chance of making that team. But almost no chance was better than no chance, which is what his odds would have been if he didn't at least try.

His was an impossible dream only made possible by having the courage to go for it.

You can double down on your strengths and shore up your weaknesses. You can surround yourself with the best people and visualize your achievements. You can do all the work and preparations and literally have a doctorate degree in who you are and what you want, but until you are willing to take a leap of faith and jump into the arena, you are just practicing. At some point, you have to be willing to get in the game.

There is a first for everything in life: first steps as a child, first day of school, first test, first game, first start, first date, etc. The only way you get to any first in your life is by taking action. It's by doing!

What causes us not to make that phone call? Not to raise our hand in class, ask that girl out, or not ask for the order? Why don't people step onto the field or into the arena of life? It's fear: fear of rejection, fear of feeling uncomfortable or embarrassed, or fear of looking foolish. But all these fears are in your own head. They are in your own imagination or from past experiences that tell you to protect yourself at all costs and not put yourself out there and take any risks.

I was much better at playing basketball in my youth than football. It probably had something to do with the fact that I was left-handed, which presented a challenge to kids trying to guard me. They couldn't figure out how to make me go to my right. I dominated opponents who tried to guard me one-on-one. Don't get me wrong; I was the starting quarterback on my junior All-American teams for three consecutive seasons. I was good in football, but I didn't really dominate like I did in basketball.

As I graduated from junior high (that's what we called middle school back in the day), the dilemma of what sport to focus on required me to choose which high school was the right fit for me. The two schools I was most interested in attending were Bishop Amat High, a Catholic football power-house, and South Hills High, which was more of a basketball school. In addition, South Hills ran the wishbone on offense, which was designed for a running quarterback, and as I've said, I was not really a runner.

The question was simple; do I want to be a basketball player or football player? It was a heavy choice for a fourteen-year-old kid. Even though I was better at basketball at the time, a voice within me indicated football would be a better choice. Maybe it was because at six feet one, I could barely touch the rim. I had no "hops." The ability to leap in basketball is pretty much a requirement, and I did not have it. So, this inner voice moved me towards football as a sport where I would have more upside.

Perfect! The decision was made. I would attend Bishop Amat to play football. Uh, not so fast!

When I applied to Amat, my parents had only paid half the tuition upfront and agreed to make the final installment during the summer before school started in September. Unfortunately, the school changed its mind for some reason when my mother showed up to make the last payment. They said, "Paul can't come here now because you didn't pay the tuition in full when it was due." We were all completely confused and shocked by the change of heart from the school. I began working more on basketball that summer because it was apparent that I would be attending South Hills. I was tremendously disappointed in this outcome.

My mother, however, is relentless when it comes to getting what she wants. She is hard to say no to. You've heard that phrase, "Acting like a dog with a bone?" That is my mom once she sets her mind to something. She went back to the high school, again and again, to beg them to let me in, and the answer was always no. So, she called upon other people to assist. She asked her great friend, Nancy Reed, a good Catholic possessing a similar bulldog mentality, to ask for a favor from the principal's boss, Bishop Juan. Bishop Juan delivered and called the principal at Bishop Amat, Fr. Zimmerman, and even he struck out!

My mom then reached out to our longtime friend Dennis Stangeland, the new freshman football coach at Amat, to apply pressure on Fr. Zimmerman. Coach Stangeland had seen me play youth football and now really wanted me to play for him. However, there was still radio silence from the school.

We had now tried direct, top-down, and bottom-up approaches to bring about our desires with no success.

Finally, during a family discussion, my mother suggested that I go to the school to talk to the principal by myself. You must understand that was a very intimidating thing for me to do. First of all, the only reason I had a chance of getting admitted to the school was that my dad was raised Catholic, so we emphasized that in the application. Non-Catholics were almost never admitted. The real story is my dad did not practice his childhood religion, and I had never attended a mass or spoken to a priest before.

As a fourteen-year-old, the thought of going to the rectory to speak directly with Fr. Zimmerman after we had been shut down for months by him was a daunting assignment, to say the least. This was especially true because he had already turned down various adults, including a Catholic bishop! How would I, just a kid, be able to convince him when they could not? I was intimidated at the thought of another rejection.

As I was processing this fear, the voice arose within me saying, "What do you have to lose, Paul?" The answer was simple—I had nothing to lose. I had nowhere to go but up.

So, I went to talk to the principal alone. I knocked on the rectory door, and another priest answered. I asked for Fr. Zimmerman, who arrived soon thereafter. I introduced myself and told him, "I want to come and be a student at Bishop Amat. Can I come?"

To my complete delight (and shock), his reply was, "You're in." That was it! There was no need for discussion or debate. No defense of my position was necessary. It was done! I was going to get to play football at Bishop Amat. Amazing!

Although I will never know for sure why Father Zimmerman said yes to me after saying no to everyone else, I believe he wanted to see me take the initiative to show him how much I wanted to attend the school. He was teaching me to advocate for myself and be accountable to my own path in life rather than having others do it for me. It was a great first life lesson for me not to be afraid to ask for the things that would help me achieve my dreams.

We can speculate about what path I would have lived if I had not had the courage to work through my fears and ask the simple question, "Can I come to school here?" I'd venture to say my world would have been completely changed, and football would not have been a part of it. By providing the answer of "very important" to the question repeated in my own mind of "How important is this to me?" I took action, and I got to live my dream life.

Tremendous possibilities do exist when we muster the

courage to give things a try. A new sale, initiating a new personal relationship, developing a new healthier body, saving or making money, and even living your childhood dream are all possible when you take that first step.

Here's the secret that not many people will tell you about having a "Go For It!" personality. What is it that's inside of them that allows them to have the courage to try things that most everybody else shies away from? It's very simple. They let it rip and then allow themselves to be okay with whatever happens. By giving themselves permission to fail, they remove the fear of failure. Instead of obsessing on the final result, they focus on doing the very best that they can and then let the chips fall where they may.

DON'T BE ATTACHED
TO AN OUTCOME

YOU DON'T HAVE TO BE A HARDCORE FAN of the
NBA to know that Kobe Bryant exuded confidence when
he stepped onto the court. So it's no surprise that, even as
a rookie, Kobe wanted the ball in his hands when the game
was on the line.

In his first season, at the ripe old age of eighteen, Kobe's
Los Angeles Lakers were down 3–1 in a best of seven Western
Conference semifinal playoff game at the Utah Jazz. With
ten seconds left and the game tied 89–89, the Lakers were
depleted. The team's starting point guard, Byron Scott, was
out of the game with an injury; its superstar center, Shaquille
O'Neal, had fouled out; and its late-game clutch shooter,
Robert Horry, was in the locker room, tossed by the refs for
getting into a scrap.[24]

The moment begged for greatness, and Kobe was ready
to supply it. With ten seconds left, he took the inbound pass

under his own hoop. With five seconds left, he paused just inside the half-court line and drove past the Jazz defender. With 1.8 seconds left, he pulled up about fifteen feet from the basket and shot a fadeaway jumper.

Pure airball.

The ball landed in the hands of Jazz power forward Karl Malone as regulation time expired, but Kobe would get another bite of the apple in overtime—actually three bites. He shot two more airballs and had the ball in his hands at the three-point line with seven seconds left and the Lakers down three. A final chance for redemption.

No such luck.

Kobe inexplicitly shot his fourth airball in a span of five minutes, and the Lakers were bounced out of the playoffs.[25] After the game, Kobe's response would define why he went on to become one of the greatest players the NBA has ever seen.

In the locker room, a group of reporters gathered in a scrum around the eighteen-year-old rookie, ready to capture what would surely be an emotional meltdown after the avalanche of airballs. They didn't get one. Without blinking an eye, Kobe simply told the reporters that he had some good looks at the basket but just didn't hit the shots.[26]

Kobe figured out at eighteen what I didn't completely understand until I was in my fifties. I needed to learn how to let go of the things that didn't go my way. And, there is no doubt these attachments held me back.

My days at USC were like something you'd read in a storybook: national championship quarterback, first-team All-American, Academic All-American, and fourth-round draft pick of the Cleveland Browns. To top it all off, my beautiful college sweetheart would go on to become my amazing life partner. Allyson and I have been married for thirty-nine years. We have four children: Michael, Stephanie, Andrew, and Matthew. We also currently have five grandchildren that bring much joy to our world.

My incredible success in college led me to believe I would replicate it in the pros. The All-American would become the All-Pro, and the college national championship would be matched with trips to the Super Bowl.

How wrong I was!

Don't misunderstand me; I really enjoyed my six years in Cleveland with the Browns and two years with the Dallas Cowboys. An eight-year career in the NFL was something to be incredibly proud of as only a small fraction of college players even have the opportunity to make it to the league. I was grateful, especially since I got to play, and I started twenty-two games during my career. However, I was also very disappointed because I didn't have the same level of success as in college. I did not win a championship, and I did not make it to the Pro Bowl.

I did lead the Browns to the playoffs in 1982 with wins over the Pittsburgh Steelers and Houston Oilers, but my big shot came in 1984 when it was my team. Cleveland Browns legend Brian Sipe, left for the USFL to play for the New Jersey Generals, and I was handed the keys to the franchise.

I realized that season when you are "the man," and countless people within the organization and outside of it are counting on you, there are tremendous expectations to perform.

Plain and simple, I played well at times, but I didn't get it done in the big moments, which is something I almost always did in college.

It was a challenge for me to understand why things unfolded the way they did that season. I reflected on it often, and my conclusion is that I tried too hard. Instead of playing relaxed and enjoying the moment, I was either thinking about being too careful so as not to make a mistake, or I was looking at the finish line too early and not focusing on the present.

Here's the thing: to perform well, you must be in the moment. Be relaxed. Play the game one play at a time for the simple love of it. I didn't do enough of those things that season.

Life is about living in the moment. Life isn't in the past or the future. The past is where limiting beliefs and traumas can reside, and the future is where the unknown exists. Life is right here, right now! We can think about and even meditate on the future we want, but we must live in the moment to maximize our experiences. When performing in school, at home, at work, or on the field, you are supposed to be living. So, be in the moment, and live.

My attachment to having a great season hampered my performance in 1984, and it affected me for years. I wondered to myself, "What would life be like today if I performed better in 1984?" If we had won more games or if we had won a championship, I thought my family would be set for life.

Some people have one foot stuck in the past and can't let go. Dwelling on past failures is a surefire way to be stuck in a negative mindset, which creates the inertia of continually repeating the same mistakes. This ultimately leads to unhappiness, and it's this unhappiness that will manifest itself in many other undesirable ways in your life.

The issue is this—there is a difference between setting goals to achieve something and placing emotional attachments to those things you desire. I was like many people who become distraught after spending weeks, months, even years in preparation for a moment to shine, and it doesn't end up the way they envisioned.

This type of emotional attachment to an outcome can greatly hamper you if you let it get out of control.

You wanted this special something for a while, a promotion, being a starter on a sports team, or going out with the man or woman of your dreams. You put in the necessary time to be prepared for this moment. You understand who you are, your strengths, your passions, and those darn limiting beliefs. You took action. You paid attention. You felt you had responded well to life's challenges. Heck, you even practiced visualization techniques to realize your desires. And yet, after expending all this time, energy, and desire—you fail.

Here is the good news—it is okay to fail!

Everyone has failed. Everyone does. Everyone will. If some of the great scientists over time didn't fail, we would not have many of the essential things that exist in society today. You might not get what you want when you want it. So what? Maybe this wasn't actually the best path for you, and maybe there is something even better around the corner that wouldn't have been there if you got what you originally wanted.

If you miss that final shot, as Kobe did, let it go and keep shooting! Remember, it's in the letting go that you receive. If you resist and dwell on the disappointment, stress will result, as well as the negative emotion created by that resistance. Always know that it is not the situation itself that creates the unhappiness; it's your reaction to it.

Have the desire to achieve great things, but do not be attached to the outcome. Just keep moving forward if you fall short. This approach to living in the moment, while also letting go of a past that didn't go your way, will allow you to enjoy life more, and it will free you up to be ready for better experiences and more opportunities that lie ahead.

TRUST THE PROCESS

THE FOUR AIRBALLS that Kobe Bryant shot in the last five minutes of a playoff game against the Utah Jazz resulted in the Lakers losing the game and getting bounced out of the playoffs. It was an inglorious way for Kobe to end his rookie season. After the game, the players and coaches boarded their team plane and arrived late at night in Los Angeles. Time to lick their wounds and get some sleep.

Not Kobe.

After landing at the airport, Kobe went straight to Palisades High, where someone opened the gym for him. While the rest of his teammates (and most Angelinos) were sleeping, Kobe took jump shot after jump shot, practicing all through the night and into the morning.[27]

This was day one of the off-season for Kobe, and he spent the rest of those months repeating the same routine he performed that evening. Go to the gym and put up the shots. After Kobe became a star in the league and no longer just a rookie trying to make his mark, the routine did not waver. Go to the gym and put up the shots.

Kobe trusted the process because the process got him there, and it kept him there. Too many other people want to take shortcuts or get instant gratification. They're looking for the lottery prize. They make weekly trips to their local convenience store to buy a ticket. They want to get rich quickly and achieve their dream overnight without putting in the work. That is the fantasy they have been sold and are living. Approximately one in three hundred million people win the Powerball or Mega Millions lottery. Do you like those odds?

Dream big and then take the time to do the work.

There is a story about Picasso sitting in a European café when a fan approached him and asked if he would draw him something on the back of a cocktail napkin. Picasso quickly obliged, but before he handed back the napkin, he asked the fan for a very large sum of money. The fan was incredulous. "How can you ask for that much? The drawing only took you a minute," to which Picasso replied, "No, It took me forty years."

Almost any big goal that you want to achieve will take time. You will have to put in the work and realize that it is a journey, not an overnight success. There is a Tom Clancy quote I love, "An overnight success is ten years in the making." Everybody wants to be a Picasso or a Kobe, but not everybody wants to do the work to get there. Here's a secret, if you love the work, it won't matter how quickly you achieve the dream because the work is the dream.

When in doubt, trust the process.

Throughout the journey, there will be times when you fall short, times when you fail. You may not shoot four airballs in front of eighteen thousand people, with millions more watching on TV, but you will have your stumbles. These are the times when self-doubt might start to creep in. We all have it, and for some, it can become paralyzing. The best response to a crisis in confidence is to go back to the basics and keep doing the work. If you stick to your plan and keep getting better, your day will come.

Kobe didn't beat himself up after missing those shots. He just went back to the gym and took more shots, like he always had before. Kobe's confidence came from knowing that all the work he had previously done made him a good player and that the bad performance was just a blip on the screen. This is why he refused to give in to what seemed like a humiliating performance. Even though he was only eighteen years old, he already knew to trust the process.

Respect the craft.

Kobe was famous for having very little patience for teammates he believed were not putting in the necessary work to earn their spot on the team. Playing in the NBA is a privilege, not a right. One of the challenges that modern society faces is an entitlement mentality where people feel like they are owed something rather than having gratitude for being given the opportunity to earn it. Not everybody has that opportunity, and it should be respected.

Imagine paying your hard-earned money to go to a concert only to find that the musicians showed up drunk and could barely play the songs you love and came to hear. Or hiring a carpenter to build you a table, but his work was so sloppy that it tilted to one side. You would lose respect for them because they didn't have respect for their craft. Right?

Respecting the craft means that the thing you love doing is so important to you that you would be embarrassed to put out a product that didn't reflect your best work. There is an honor to knowing that your craft, one of the things that makes you special, came about because you were willing to do the work to be the best you can be at it.

After Kobe tragically died in a helicopter crash, there was much talk in the media about the "mamba mentality." Nicknamed the Black Mamba, the mamba mentality referenced Kobe's strong mindset and deep passion for trying to become the very best basketball player on the planet.

The extraordinary competitiveness that stirred within Kobe resulted in him winning five NBA championships, two Olympic gold medals, two NBA Finals MVP awards, one regular-season MVP, two NBA scoring championships, eighteen NBA All-Star appearances, and fourth on the all-time NBA scoring list. It is a basketball career resume only matched by a very small handful of players.

With all those accomplishments, it is interesting to see what Kobe said at the Staples Center ceremony when his numbers (8 and 24) were retired by the Lakers. "Those times when you get up early and you work hard. Those times you stay up late and you work hard. Those times when you don't feel like working. You're too tired. You don't want to push yourself, but you do it anyway. That is actually the dream."[28]

Living the dream.

The process is the dream. When you find those things in life that you love doing, you will enjoy the journey. Ask yourself a simple question. Do you think Kobe loved basketball?

I think we all know that the answer is an easy yes. However, notice that I didn't ask, did he love *playing* basketball.

It is easy to love being on the court and playing the game, but to be the best, are you willing to do the other stuff that makes you the best? Often the things we love to do have ancillary responsibilities or exercises that must be completed, which, quite frankly, we don't always enjoy. However, those are the sacrifices we must make to live our dream.

It is clear that Kobe loved basketball, but when he talked about doing the hard work, he acknowledged that there were times when he felt tired or didn't really want to push himself, but he did it anyway. Why? Because he loved basketball so much, he had a respect for the craft. That respect grew into a love for perfecting the craft because participating in that journey made it possible for him to do the thing he loved so much—playing basketball. And he knew that if he trusted the process, good things would follow. That is the dream.

TRUST THE FLOW

WHEN KOBE BRYANT SHOT all of those airballs in the playoff game against Utah, he didn't get down on himself; he just went back to work that same night. He trusted the process. He knew that if you put in the work, day by day, every day, the work will pay off.

Sometimes it pays off in ways you didn't initially plan for.

The next step beyond trusting the process is trusting the flow. This means that when things don't go according to your plan, you trust that something better might replace your previous expectations. However, it's not always easy to accept that new curve in the road.

As an example, put yourself in this position and be honest with how you would react.

You have played in the NBA for eleven years. During that span, you have started 806 straight games, never coming off the bench. You have made the All-Rookie Team, the All-Star Team, and the All-Defensive Team. Last season you were signed to a four-year contract worth $48 million—a reward for being one of the best players in the league.[29]

This season you have a new coach, and during the preseason, the new guy tells you that he would like you to give up your starter role and lead the second unit, which comes off the bench. And, oh, by the way, the new coach is a rookie who has never coached a regular-season game in the NBA (or in college, for that matter).[30]

You can imagine that many NBA players, with egos bigger than their outsized basketball frames, might tell the rookie coach where to stick that idea.

Andre Iguodala had two ways to react when his new coach Steve Kerr offered his suggestion. He could get totally stressed out and view his new role as a demotion that signaled his NBA career was on a downward spiral, or he could accept the role as a new challenge that would help the team reach its goal of winning its first NBA championship. It should be noted that Iguodala had never yet made it to the NBA finals.

Iguodala chose to be the consummate professional, let go of his ego, and accept his new status as the team's sixth man. The rest is history. That season the Warriors won their first championship in forty years, and Iguodala was the NBA Finals MVP![31] During the five-year span after accepting Kerr's decision, Iguodala played a key role on a Warriors team that made the NBA finals in five straight seasons and won three championships. Downward spiral indeed.

Iguodala trusted that a new way, even one that might be perceived as a demotion, could lead to better results. Honestly, most players in his shoes would have probably been attached to their identity as a starter and not able to accept their new role. But here's the thing, attachment to things that are lost and can't be changed is a surefire way to be unhappy, create stress, and prohibit your growth.

The inability to accept changes in your life can cause high stress and anxiety. Oftentimes it is the reaction to a challenge in life, and not the challenge itself, that causes people to spin out of control and become unhealthy. For example, a person loses their job and compounds the problem by getting sick with anxiety or making poor choices that prohibit them from getting a new job.

The flip side of the coin of attachment is acceptance. Acceptance frees us up. It allows us to unburden ourselves from past hurts and disappointments. Many people can't accept the negative things that happened in their lives and continue to rage against injustices that have long since passed. Or, they can't accept that other people have achieved something that they believe more rightfully belongs to them.

Acceptance creates space for us to receive new opportunities in our lives and let go of the ones that weren't meant to be. If you constantly dwell on and think about what didn't go your way and what didn't happen for you that you had envisioned, then you are trapped. There is no room for other good things to enter your being, your space.

Imagine a water glass. If you keep pouring the same old stuff into it, hurts from your past and disappointments, the glass will overflow with negativity. This is a victim state, which can trap you into perpetual unhappiness.

Conversely, if you are more accepting and let go of past traumas and current stressful situations, room is left in the glass to pour more fresh cold water. There is room now for the good, the positive to come to you.

This is an empowered state. It's in the letting go that we receive!

When my NFL playing career was over, I needed to transition from football to business. Although my head was ready to accept the transition and let go of my past career, in retrospect, my heart was not. I bounced from one investment company to the next with varying degrees of success and then found myself involved in a few different entrepreneurial ventures that were less than successful. I was just surviving, not thriving.

We even had to move out of our house a couple of times and rent it to make ends meet. We moved in with my in-laws, Roger and Marilyn, who were gracious hosts, but it was very humbling for me, as you might imagine. We now had three children, and my wife was on edge and not pleased with the situation, which added to the stress level.

Thirteen years had passed since I retired from the game, and I was still very unsure of my next chapter. I was searching for a job/career that I had a passion for, where I would have fulfillment in my work as I had in football.

This search landed me in the commercial title insurance industry with a renewed vigor and motivation. I had solid success and, with a robust commercial real estate market, I was making good money. The business required a lot of entertaining by the sales executives. And so I entertained and won some significant business, which was great! My USC history, Trojan broadcasting duties, and connections certainly made a big difference. I finally found the vehicle that would lead to financial success and freedom.

And yet, I was still unhappy.

My new endeavor required me to be out for dinner and drinks on many evenings with prospects and clients. Also, business trips were commonplace, so there was more going out, more drinking, more late nights with clients and prospects. After several years of this frenetic business lifestyle, I woke up in Las Vegas with a bad hangover one morning. Staring at myself in the hotel room mirror, I realized I didn't like what I had become.

Even though I was doing well financially, there was still something missing inside me. I didn't know it at the time, but I was still searching. I was tired of playing the game, and I wanted to find Paul, the real Paul. That's when I stopped chasing things, chasing jobs, chasing a career. I turned inward for answers and drove to the desert loaded with deep questions and many books, CDs, and DVDs to digest.

As I dove into who I was and what I wanted, I began to evaluate the things that brought me joy and peace in my life. I came to realize that it was not my job that I disliked; it was my approach that made me unhappy.

It was time to get into the flow and to trust that flow! It was time to allow things to happen for me instead of forcing them to happen. It was time to stop trying to control life and to start living it by letting go. So, I began to let go of past mistakes, past what-ifs, and my timetable for what I deemed to be a successful life. The focus on chasing numerical goals, whether sales goals for the company or personal goals for my bank account, were a big source of who I thought I was supposed to be, and it was time to let go.

I had been holding on to that approach for far too long. When you do so, there is tension between you and the universe (Life), like a taut and stiff rope. This tension creates discontent, discord, and probably dis-ease (aka stress), but when you release that tension and relax, it opens a portal to the flow or fluidity of life, which allows for new opportunities to present themselves. These new opportunities are presented because you are now open to a new way of thinking, a new life that leads to peace within.

My new way of thinking was to quit trying to force my way to success but instead to allow the things I naturally loved doing to lead me there. The part of the job I loved was my ability to build relationships with people, help them with their needs, and connect them to other people who could also help them. I stopped looking at the numbers and began to trust that being a person whose mission to love and serve others would lead me to success.

It worked!

I never did better than when I trusted that doing things the right way would create a positive flow and eventually circle back to me. Instead of stressing that meeting with clients had to translate into instant sales, my approach was to view life with gratitude for the things that I already had, to know that there is an abundance that would allow me to continue thriving, and to trust that things would work out, even when they veered from my plans.

You might have expectations of what your life should look like today, and it's not working out as planned. Stay conscious and pay attention to the messaging you've been receiving. If you feel like you love what you are doing in all phases of life, then keep moving down the path. Trust in the next bend. Trust in the next minute, hour, and day of your life and believe that when you've been thrown a curveball, there is something even better around the next corner.

Trust the flow and understand that the flow isn't just your career; it's your life and every component of it. As an example, my son Andrew dreamed of playing quarterback in the Pac-12, but that didn't work out. He ended up starting for New Mexico State, a Group of Five school. This is where he met Elise, the love of his life and future wife—a much better outcome than he ever dreamed of.

We all must believe and trust that every step in our life is moving us in a more favorable direction for our overall human evolution, our life's purpose! If you operate your life in this manner, this trust in the flow will also enhance your confidence in all things you pursue because it won't just be you driving it. It will be a power beyond your understanding.

True faith is the greatest source of true confidence, and it is the most important thing that will get you through some of life's most challenging moments.

V. GRIT

*View your challenges as experiences that
make you stronger and help you grow*

THE ONE THING
WE CAN CONTROL

YOU'VE TAKEN THE NECESSARY ACTIONS to create your best self. You've made the changes to put yourself on the right track. You've worked hard to expand upon your strengths and shore up your weaknesses. You're chugging along on this great path that you've created, and then a major obstacle comes crashing down.

Sometimes you do everything right, but something completely out of your control knocks you down.

My youngest son, Matthew, was the starting quarterback as a junior at a Southern California high school football powerhouse, Mater Dei. He beat out a young phenom in training camp to win the job and was 1–0 heading into week two. The expectations to perform as "the guy" were enormous. This was a program that has a rich history of winning championships, high national rankings, and Heisman Trophy-winning quarterbacks, like John Huarte and Matt Leinart.

Despite the level of pressure that came with the job, Matthew was managing everything very well. His parents were not! Sitting in the stands was nerve-racking, to say the least. We all want our kids to perform well, have success, and be happy, right?

Matthew was off to a decent start in the second game when something completely shocking happened. He was flushed out of the pocket on a pass play, and he escaped to his left. While avoiding defenders, he jumped in the air to loft a ball to one of his receivers, which barely fell incomplete. We looked over to see if Matthew was okay after being flattened to the turf. He wasn't.

After he got up, Matthew jetted to the sideline, with his left arm dangling at his side, and went directly to the trainer. I immediately went to the field to see how he was doing. It was noticeably clear that Matthew was injured. The preliminary diagnosis by the team doctor was a broken left wrist.

Everything he had worked for went up in smoke on that one ill-fated play.

Allyson and I rushed him to the nearest hospital, where Elise, our middle son Andrew's girlfriend at the time, worked as a nurse. She was able to get him right through emergency and into a room where X-rays were taken and an examination was performed. Our worst fears became a reality. It was a fractured left wrist! After the doctor set the arm, he put it in a splint, and we went home.

It was an emotional night for the entire McDonald family. The good news was no surgery was required, and the injury sustained was to his non-throwing arm. This trauma to the body wasn't just physical. It was mental, and it was emotional. We now knew Matthew's football future was unknown. It was difficult watching Matthew's dream of getting a scholarship to play college football possibly taken away, but that was a possibility we knew we had to face.

To the inexperienced observer, an injury during your high school junior year of football should not be cause for major concern. Even if you miss the season, you still have your entire senior season to look forward to, right? Well, it's more complicated than that.

In the crazy world of college sports recruiting, it is extremely important to have success early in high school. This allows plenty of time for college coaches to get to know the players they want to come to their school. Also, the theory within the recruiting system suggests there is a trajectory of growth and improved performance by these athletes of interest. So, if they are good when they are younger, then they can only get better.

In general, there is a finite window of opportunity whereby the athlete must show their goods on the field or court. The bottom line is that if you haven't received scholarship offers by the end of your junior season, it will be a steep mountain to climb for you even to be looked at by any Division 1 (D-1) college recruiter. Matthew was a junior, and we now knew that the season was essentially lost due to his injury. He would only have one year to prove his worth, assuming we could get a school to pay attention since his recruiting window was essentially closed.

Case in point, I was fortunate to start a couple of games as a sophomore in high school and received attention from college coaches because I played so well when I was younger. During my junior year, I was the full-time starter but sustained an injury in the last game of the regular season. This injury did not affect the interest from colleges because I had, by then, a lot of tape for the coaches to see my ability. Matthew only had one game. Also, these coaches had invested a good amount of their time in me to know I would be a great fit for their program.

So, what do you do if an injury were to happen? How do you respond? To put it simply, you get back to work.

I give full credit to Andrew, Matthew's older brother by eight years, for immediately recognizing this and wasting very little time lamenting the bad fortune. Andrew was a warrior, and his road to being a starting quarterback at New Mexico State was always a challenge. He had to fight for everything he achieved in sports, so it was his idea to get Matthew back to work, splint and all.

The injury occurred on a Friday in early September, and Matthew was training the following Wednesday on his core and legs to improve his speed, quickness, and athleticism. Matthew started working out with the same guy, Brent Concolino, that trained Andrew ten years earlier.

It wasn't only Matthew working out with Brent. He was joined by Andrew and Michael, the eldest brother, who played quarterback for USC. The old man also joined the party. We all got up at 5:30 AM, four days a week, so that Matthew could get in his workout prior to school starting. We were on this same program for two months when he was finally cleared to practice.

The results—when Matthew returned to the field, he was faster and more athletic than before his injury. He could have felt sorry for himself and did nothing, which would have been the expected thing to do in his situation. But, he got back to work and continued to hone his craft to get better despite this significant setback. We were all proud of him for stepping up at a very challenging time in his young life.

There is an infinite number of variables available in the world in which we live. Do we control how fast the earth travels through space, or whether it will rain next month, or what your boss will say to you at work tomorrow? If you are an athlete, do you have control of if/when you sustain an injury?

The answer to all the above is no!

We have zero control over anything in our lives except one thing: how we respond to any given situation. We can't control what happens in the world, but we can control our reactions to it. That is the only thing we have absolute control over.

There are many people in this world who have been placed into a really bad situation through no fault of their own. Maybe it's you. It really sucks to have to deal with so much crap that you know other people do not deal with. It is natural and fair to be angry. You have a right to be angry, but at some point, constantly complaining about your bad luck will start to define who you are.

There comes a time when you have to accept you have been dealt an unfair hand and that simply complaining about your bad luck won't make things any better for you. You have to decide that you will do everything in your power to create a path from your poor circumstances to a better place. The key word here is power.

The late John Lewis was one of the most powerful people that our nation has ever produced. Lewis was one of the original thirteen Freedom Riders who fought for racial justice during the civil rights struggles in the 1960s. The Freedom Riders were made up of White and Black young people who rode together on a bus from Washington, DC, to New Orleans to protest the segregation laws in various Southern states that prohibited mixed races from sitting next to each other on public transportation.[32]

Lewis and his fellow riders were often jailed and beaten by mobs during the trek, but they continued. During one beating in Montgomery, Alabama, Lewis was hit over the head with a wooden crate and left unconscious on the ground of a bus station.[33] Although Lewis was a victim of crimes and ugly racist hatred, he would not allow himself to become a victim of life. Quite the opposite. With every beating he endured, Lewis became more powerful, and through his power and the powers of others, the segregation policies in the South were overturned.

Lewis was later elected to the United States Congress, where he served from 1987 to 2020, the year he died.[34] Although the racism that Lewis spent his entire life fighting still existed to the day he died, he never gave in and accepted it as just the way things are. His power came from his willingness to fight for a more just society. The struggle might never end, but the power comes from the decision to do something about the injustice rather than accept just being a victim of it.

Empowered people create the life they want! Lewis wanted to be a part of a society where segregation laws are overturned, and that is exactly what he did. We have a choice about how we respond to our environment and anything in life that is presented to us. If we are powerful beings, then we can certainly control our actions to direct our personal lives and/or society into the paths we choose.

Being negative or positive is a choice. I propose we choose positivity!

Not all of us do something as epic as Lewis and his Freedom Riders did to change the laws in the South. But every one of our lives should be viewed as a miracle that is worth living, and in our own way, as epic. We have everyday interactions with friends, family, co-workers, and classmates where our words and actions can have a ripple effect. Be mindful of that.

Is the ripple that you are creating positive or negative?

Take control and note what you are thinking and saying to yourself and others. Redirect your perspective to a more positive outlook even if in the beginning you are playing a game and pretending to be positive. If you continue choosing to be positive and upbeat, a new habit will develop over time, and you will slowly reprogram yourself to have a personal power that might have previously been lacking.

We all have our own challenges and our own dreams. Whether other people think they are small or large, important or inconsequential, they are everything to us. Don't let other people define what is important to you or what you can or can't achieve. The power to make those choices are yours.

Matthew's dream from the time he was a small boy was to get a scholarship to play college football. His broken wrist posed a major challenge to achieving that dream, which he immediately responded to by getting into a training routine that made him stronger and faster.

However, another challenge emerged. It became clear that Matthew would probably not have the opportunity to get back his starting quarterback position for his senior year. He could not control his coach's decision, so he needed to figure out a new path to keep his dream alive. He could have stayed put and likely been a backup during his senior year and hope to showcase his abilities on a community college team, or he could transfer to another high school to accelerate the process by being the starter his senior year.

The family guided Matthew in his decision, but ultimately, it was his call. It was a difficult decision. He had spent almost three years at Mater Dei making great friends among his team-mates and classmates. His transferring meant being the new kid in school for his senior year. Although it meant starting over, Matthew was resolute in his decision to get back on his path and continue pursuing his dream, so he transferred. It ended up being a great choice.

In his senior season at Mission Viejo High School, Matthew threw thirty-nine touchdowns and ran for four more, leading the team to the quarterfinals of the playoffs. Matthew took full control of his destiny, and it paid off. His performance that season created an opportunity to continue playing on a full-ride scholarship at Boston College, one of the top universities in the nation!

CHALLENGES
ARE GOOD

MY SON MATTHEW TOOK CONTROL of the challenge put in front of him and put himself in the best possible position to achieve his goal of earning a scholarship to play college football at a D-1 school. But it was not easy. It was a huge commitment and took considerable time and effort to deliver the game performances at his new high school.

When I asked Matthew about his mindset when deciding to transfer to another school, he admitted that he had a big chip on his shoulder. I asked him, "Weren't you motivated before?" He responded, "Not like this!"

One of the purposes a challenge serves is to compel us to answer this question, "How badly do I want it?" Or, stated another way, "How important is this to me?" Matthew answered this question loudly and clearly by putting in all the necessary extra work to create a stellar season.

Playing football was incredibly important to him, and he was rewarded with the opportunity to continue doing his thing in college as a scholarship football player.

Ironically, Matthew wasn't the only one in the family to suffer a bad break during their high school football career. I also had a significant challenge during my junior season in high school. The last game of the season, Bishop Amat played our top rival to determine the league championship. I wasn't feeling well with a significant cough (that later turned into pneumonia), and I was a bit rundown; however, I wasn't about to miss this game.

We were moving the ball easily down the field early in the game, and I was feeling better than expected, probably due to my adrenaline rush. While facing a third and six on about our own forty-yard line, I dropped back to pass and found a running back open in the underneath coverage. As the ball released from my hand, someone landed on my right leg, and I felt a significant pop. I went down immediately in a great deal of pain. I knew it was not good!

I was carried off the field and stayed on the sideline after the doctor checked my knee. He told me I was done for the game. But, what I didn't know was the long haul I was in for— three surgeries with two large screws inserted in my knee and a yearlong recovery to make it back to the field.

This was the first significant setback I experienced in sports. Throughout my youth, things happened quickly and easily for me as I was generally one of the stars of the teams I played on in basketball and football. As a sophomore in high school, I started a couple of games and threw three touchdown passes in one of them, which, as I mentioned, caught the eye of Paul Hackett, quarterback coach for the Cal Bears. Soon thereafter, Paul and the Cal coaches started the recruiting process and wanted me to join their program. Everything was falling into place as I entered that last regular-season game in November.

Suddenly, things got a lot more challenging!

The sports medicine surgeon who performed the operations told me that because the break in three places of the right femur occurred in the growth plate area of the joint, there was a chance my right leg would be shorter than my left leg. This was a scary statement because it could impede my athletic progress and my chances of playing college football. Life had just thrown me a curveball when I was always hitting fastballs out of the park.

How was I going to react?

For a few weeks after the first surgery, I was down in the dumps. I felt sorry for myself because nothing like this had ever happened to me. I had never experienced any sort of setback in sports or life as I was always on a consistent upward trajectory. However, I came to realize that I didn't have time to wallow in my misfortune of what had already happened. I needed to stay present and deal with reality by hitting my rehabilitation like no other if I were to ever step on the field again.

Through this process, I learned how to deal with adversity in my life for the very first time. Did I like it? No, I did not. But, I made it through because I loved football so much I would endure just about anything to be able to keep playing. This focused effort and commitment paid off as I finally made it back as the full-time starter midway through my senior year, where we made it to the playoffs. The next stop was USC.

My head coach at the Cleveland Browns, Sam Rutigliano, used to say, "You have to play the hand you are dealt." So, once you get over whatever negative situation occurred in your life, you start the process to move through it. You adjust! You play your hand to the best of your ability, and you move on to the next hand in your life.

After recovering, I realized that moving through my broken leg led me to understand life a little better. To understand that life doesn't always go our way. To understand potholes and speed bumps may be around the corner waiting for us, and we never see them coming.

My injury experience in high school helped me know how to better manage being fired three times in two years in the NFL, as well as multiple career and job changes later in life. It allowed me to know that being flexible by going with the flow is one of the most important ways to live a peaceful, confident, and productive life.

Please know that I'm aware many people face much steeper challenges in life than a broken leg. They might have been born with a major medical issue or were raised in a household that was afflicted with drug addiction or poverty. But if you ask people who came out the other side of those negative experiences to become productive and joyful members of society if they would change their past, a large majority of them would say no.

Why? Because all their experiences, good and bad, are what have molded them into who they are. The painful experiences are often the ones they cite as being the most important in guiding them to become high-quality people. Their challenges made them better.

One of the important things about challenges is that they teach us lessons that allow us to grow, so we can improve as a human being. I believe we are here on this planet to evolve. It doesn't matter at what level we enter this dimension; the message is to grow from that point in maturity, wisdom, and what we give to others. Do we grow and evolve much when things are going great? NO, we don't. We grow when we are faced with challenges that we are able to move through.

So, if we are here to grow and evolve as human beings, and we do so when we experience challenges, then challenges are GOOD! I use the word challenge instead of difficulties, hard times, or any number of other "negative" words because it better describes something that can be overcome.

This leads to the discussion on language: words, written and spoken, and thoughts are enormously powerful in life. How we think, what we say, and write influence what we do, and consequently, how we live. We must always be cognizant, be conscious of what we are telling ourselves.

So, how do we monitor the millions of thoughts we have each day? We do so by knowing how we are feeling. If we are feeling good, we must be thinking good thoughts. If we are feeling poorly, then we must be having negative thoughts. So, if we are feeling poorly, we need to consciously rethink, restate, rewrite who we are and how we live to feel better! Do not underestimate the power of language and words in our daily lives.

Your greatest power in life will come from the challenges you have moved through with resolve and commitment. These experiences will elevate you to greater heights, build internal belief for each subsequent obstacle to be overcome, and will help you to truly start understanding that miracles are possible—even when the challenges that appear are bigger than you could have ever imagined.

NO ACCIDENTS,
ONLY MIRACLES

THE IRONMAN TRIATHLON IN HAWAII is one of the most strenuous endurance races ever invented. The race starts with a 2.4-mile swim in the ocean waters of Kailua-Kona Bay on the Big Island of Hawaii. After getting out of the water, contestants hop on a bike for a 112-mile ride across a Hawaiian lava desert, and the race concludes with a marathon-length run (twenty-six miles) along the island coast.

Now, imagine completing this grueling race on two prosthetic legs. Well, after October 12, 2019, you wouldn't have to imagine it anymore. On that date, Roderick Sewell became the first above-the-knee double amputee to complete the Hawaii Ironman race on prosthetics. To make this amazing story even more miraculous, Roderick not only overcame his disability to become a world-class athlete, but he also spent a number of his childhood years homeless.[35]

Roderick was born with the tibia bone missing in both of his legs. More popularly known as a shinbone, Roderick's rare condition forced his mother, Marian Jackson, to make an extremely difficult decision. Roderick explained, "She decided to get my legs amputated at age one and a half. I got my first pair of prosthetics at age three, and just kind of took off from there."[36]

Marian tried from a very young age to instill a sense of independence in Roderick, and so when he left his bottle in the corner of a room, she would make him crawl to get it for himself instead of retrieving it for him. "He got used to everybody catering to him," explained Marian. "I'm like no. You want that bottle? Go get it." Roderick added, "She knew I could. She knew it would be beneficial for me and that the world wouldn't hold my hand when it came to getting what I wanted."[37]

As Roderick began learning to use his prosthetics, it became apparent that the low-grade model that Marian's health insurance provided wasn't going to be sufficient for him to enjoy a normal lifestyle. They were clunky and would easily break. The costs of prosthetics were extremely high, and Marian felt her best option was to quit her job so that Roderick's prosthetics could be covered by medical insurance that the state of California provided.[38]

"She was doing pretty well on her own, but when they told her the price of the prosthetics, she told them she couldn't afford it. The fastest route she could think of was to quit her job, file for unemployment, and get full coverage for my prosthetics," said Roderick. He added, "So because of her sacrifice I was able to walk."

It was a steep sacrifice—quitting her job for Roderick to get decent prosthetics caused deep economic hardship for the family. Their financial situation continued to worsen, and they eventually found themselves homeless and forced to sleep in shelters. "I cried all the time," said Marian. She added, "I tried to make it into an adventure. I had to ease him into it because he couldn't understand why we couldn't go home."

To make matters worse, Marian and Roderick were sometimes forced to sleep in shelters that gave them no privacy. Marian explained what her life was like when she was among people that she feared could harm her child. "You don't sleep. It was awful and with me being the parent of an amputee child, you can't leave the room for safety reasons."

Understandably, Roderick's self-esteem was at a really low point during these years. He felt very self-conscious about what other kids thought of his prosthetics, and there were times when the African-American young man also experienced racism. These negative experiences were all compounded by the extreme strain of being homeless. However, one day, when Marian and Roderick were getting off the trolley, someone approached them and asked if he might be interested in signing up for sports with the Challenged Athletes Foundation (CAF).

Roderick found himself playing various sports in competitions sponsored by CAF, including wheelchair basketball, hand cycling, running, and wheelchair soccer. Playing sports changed Roderick's life. He said, "I was ten when I got my first running blades. I was still homeless, but walking around with a smile on my face because I had a new outlet, a new way of life, and it was being active, doing sports."

Through the CAF, Roderick would eventually meet one of his best friends, Rudy Garcia-Tolson. Rudy was already on his way to becoming an accomplished swimmer when they met (he later captured three Paralympic gold medals and two silver medals). He asked Roderick if he wanted to try swimming. Although Roderick had a fear of water, his new buddy inspired him to give it a try. Marian recalled the transformation that occurred when Roderick began swimming. "Once he got out there he felt freedom, no prosthetics, no nothing, he could swim. He felt free."

Roderick got a late start in competitive swimming and, at first, was the underdog that everybody rooted for at swim meets. Marian recalled one of his first competitions. "You could see him struggling to get across that pool. It was taking another two or three minutes." She laughed and added, "But he kept going and that was the biggest thing for him, it was to just finish."

As Roderick's swimming career progressed, he incredibly went from struggling to finish a race to becoming a world-class para-athletics swimmer. He ultimately made the United States swim team and won the gold medal in the two hundred-meter breaststroke final of the Para-Pan Games, an international adaptive sports competition for all North and South American nations.

Roderick's gold medal and the historic accomplishment of being the first double amputee to complete the Hawaii Ironman are amazing accomplishments, but when asked if these achievements are how he'd like to be known, Roderick said no and instead pointed to his resilience as the quality that most accurately defines him. "I see a lot of people, limbs or no limbs, who have kind of given up on life and I could have easily been one of those people. Thankfully I had my support group and them pushing me is helping me break boundaries, break barriers, and break stereotypes like, 'Oh, Black people can't swim,' or 'If you're an amputee, you can't do anything,' all these different things that you could listen to if you wanted to, but I just refuse to be held back."[4]

Roderick embodies a philosophy that I try to live by, "No Accidents, Only Miracles." It's not always easy. Life can throw you some pretty challenging curveballs. Consider being born with the one in a million misfortune of having no shinbones. That's not tough enough? Okay, let's throw in a childhood where you spend many years sleeping in homeless shelters. But here's the thing; all of these "accidents" of life made Roderick who he is, a miracle.

There are no coincidences in life. This may be a difficult subject to wrap your head around when something traumatic happens to you or to the life of a loved one. You must understand that everyone is on their own unique path and that sometimes this path is incomprehensible.

Many people believe that life happens to them and they have no control over it (victim state). Because of this perspective, we are not empowered. If we come at life from an empowered state, then every experience (positive or negative) is a worthy one, no matter what happens, because it is meant for our overall "evolve-ment" as a human.

Remember, we can't control what happens to us, but we can control our reaction to it!

If something difficult happens in our life, or something we worked really hard for doesn't come to fruition, we tend to get upset, despondent, disappointed, or angry (victim state). And so, someone coming from a negative or victim state may say, "It's no accident that this happened to me because my life sucks!" From an empowered state, we trust the flow of life, so we say, "There must be something better for us up next."

If you genuinely believe something good is in the process of happening for you right around the corner, it will appear in some shape or form at some time. Be aware and pay attention to what is being presented to you since all experiences in your life matter.

If something that we've been working on or planning for does happen, it is our own little (or big) miracle. These miracles, big and small, are things that we should always remember to be grateful for. And, interestingly, the more gratitude we have, the more miracles we start to notice and experience. However, "Only Miracles" doesn't just apply to achieving the things we desire. Oftentimes we seek out one thing and don't get it, but because our path gets redirected, we end up receiving something else. Maybe it's something better; maybe it's not. But, whatever the case, it is a miracle, and having gratitude will keep those miracles coming!

Oftentimes we believe that the miracles we are seeking don't happen fast enough. Why do we always want to fast forward to the finish line? It's because we believe knowing our outcome will relieve the stress of living. I am here to tell you—it will not! We will always want more because that is what drives our ego. And, what fun would it be anyway to know an outcome before it happens? It's in the excitement of not knowing that makes life worth living. It is the surprises, both positive and negative, that shape us. We are more elated when something good occurs unexpectedly, and we have more opportunities to grow through unforeseen challenges.

I can't imagine challenges much greater than Roderick Sewell's, where he had both legs cut off above the kneecap before he was two years old and was homeless for years bouncing from shelter to shelter. But, look at him today. He is an accomplished, medal-winning, global athlete who travels the world to compete in the sports he loves.

Roderick also has an opportunity to share his story. His miracle creates awareness that other people have the power to create their own unique personal miracles. I saw this first-hand when Roderick was competing and mentoring athletes at UCLA in the Angel City Games, a premiere festival for adaptive sports. Kids and adult athletes with prosthetics all gravitated toward Roderick and his magnetic smile.

Roderick is keenly aware of how the challenges he has faced give him the unique opportunity to guide others that are like him. "You know, when they come up to me and I tell them people are gonna think you can't do something. You can either let them tell you what to do or you can do your own thing. You can do what drives you and that's one thing I let them know, don't let somebody else put restrictions on you," explained Roderick.

If someone had told the young Roderick, a double amputee sleeping on a cot in a shelter, that he was a miracle, he might not have believed it. But, we can all now see what a miracle he truly is. Winning a gold medal and finishing the Ironman race are truly miraculous accomplishments for Roderick. Still, the most miraculous thing is how his overcoming the "accidents" of his life can now serve as an inspiration to show so many people that miracles are possible.

Just like Roderick, you have the power within to create miracles. Always keep smiling, have fun on your journey, and trust in the flow of what comes your way. We live in an abundant universe, and those miracles can manifest in magical ways if we have the courage to believe.

VI. COURAGE

Have the courage to be vulnerable and face your challenges

MOVING PAST FEAR

MAGICAL.

Do a Google search of "Coco Gauff Wimbledon," and magical is the word that appears in headline after headline to describe Coco's historic run through the 2019 Wimbledon tennis tournament. The magic started in the very first round when Coco faced Venus Williams. Coco was a fifteen-year-old girl staring across the net at her tennis idol, a woman who had previously won seven Grand Slam singles championships, including five at Wimbledon, and a gold medal in singles at the 2000 Summer Olympics at Sydney. This was Coco's first Wimbledon.[39]

In a stunning display, which became the most talked about match of the tournament, Coco played nearly flawless tennis in defeating her legendary idol. Ironically, it was Venus who struggled, committing twenty-six unforced errors, which Coco coolly took advantage of by converting all three of her break opportunities on the way to a 6–4, 6–4 victory.

Coco went on to win her next two matches, which put her in the Round of 16, where she lost to eventual champion Simona Halep 6–3, 6–3. To put that into perspective, Halep went on to win the next three matches without losing a set, including a 6–2, 6–2 thrashing of Venus's sister, Serena, in the tournament final.

At fifteen years old, Coco was the youngest player to win a match at Wimbledon in twenty-eight years. She defeated her idol, a legend in the tennis world, and, along her journey throughout the tournament, Coco captured the hearts and minds of sports fans around the world.[40]

It almost didn't happen.

About a year before the Wimbledon tournament, where Coco's performance would serve as a great inspiration to so many people, she herself had lost her inspiration to play. *USA Today* reported on a piece that Coco wrote about her battle with depression on the website *Behind the Racquet*, "Right before Wimbledon, going back around 2017/18, I was struggling to figure out if this is what I really wanted."[41]

Coco was one of the most acclaimed players in all of junior tennis, with the promise of an amazing career laid out right in front of her. You would think knowing that would have given her the confidence to want to get up every day and continue on her path to greatness. However, it was precisely that expectation that began to hold her back.

Anxiety, which came from the hype of being a rising tennis star, almost forced Coco to take a hiatus from tennis. The game that she loved so much was no longer fun to play. *USA Today* quoted part of Coco's post in *Behind the Racquet*:

"Throughout my life, I was always the youngest to do things, which added hype that I didn't want. It added this pressure that I needed to do well fast."[42]

Coco came to realize that for her to be able to enjoy tennis, she could not let the pressure of other people's expectations burden her. Coco explained what she had figured out, "I realized I needed to start playing for myself, not other people."[43] She also said, "Once I let that all go, that's when I started to have the results I wanted."[44]

Although Coco is a uniquely talented tennis player, her fear of needing to live up to a perceived standard of perfection is not that unique. A research survey commissioned by Procter & Gamble found that the pressure to be perfect and the social perceptions of others contributed to a fear of failure that is especially prevalent among young ladies.

The 2017 study found that during puberty, 50 percent of girls felt paralyzed by a fear of failure, 70 percent avoided trying new things because they were afraid to fail. Sixty percent said failing made them want to quit, 80 percent reported that societal pressure to please others contributed to their fear of failure, 75 percent agreed that social media contributed to that pressure, and over 80 percent acknowledged that if they felt failing was acceptable, they would have kept doing the things they loved and grew in confidence.[45]

It is sad to see how prevalent the fear of failure is among young ladies. However, fear is not gender-specific. It is also not age-specific. We all have it, and fear of failure is not the only one.

There are numerous fears: fear of rejection, fear of losing control, fear of change, fear of missing out, fear of poverty, and fear of death. These are just a few examples of what can hold us back.

Like many people, I have had many fears in my lifetime. The fear of not providing for my family and the fear of making a mistake are two that jump out. However, my biggest challenge has always been the fear of not being good enough.

I was a very good student, earning As and Bs throughout my childhood, high school, and college studies. I remember coming home from school excited to share my excellent report card of four As and one B with my mom. She looked at the card and said, "Good job, Paul, but what happened with this B?" Wow! I felt disappointed because all the focus was on where I didn't live up to expectations—and the expectations were high!

Fast forward to the profession and position I chose to play—a quarterback in football. It's interesting how this same kind of critique followed me to my first career—a career where you are only as good as your last game, or even your last play. The focus in the film room is almost always on what you did wrong or what you need to do better. The coach may spend what seems like ten minutes on all your good plays and an hour on your three poor plays.

I get it. Coaches and parents are there to instruct and correct behaviors. This is how you don't repeat the same mistakes. However, an overemphasis on the negative can lead to an obsession with what you didn't do correctly. It can flood your mind with the bad when you should always be focusing on the good, allowing for "more good" to happen on the field and in life.

This "more good" mindset can also avoid the pitfalls of the destructive cycle of perfectionism. The fear of not being good enough is something I have had to overcome. It is what drove me to take the first step to rediscover myself by traveling to the desert to spend a few days on a personal retreat of self-reflection. I was taking a big risk and stepping into uncharted waters. Even though it changed me forever for the better, the fear of not being good enough still occasionally rears its ugly head, and I have to say to myself, "I am good enough" to move through this feeling of inadequacy.

What about you? Do you feel that your fears hold you back from the things you want to accomplish and the relationships you want to have? Are you negative much of the time?

This state of being will slowly disintegrate the energy within you, the energy of who you truly are designed to be— your authentic self. I suggest you begin to recognize this negativity and shift your perspective to the positive by focusing on the good. Focus on what you do well. Focus on what brings you joy. This new mindset will help you have the courage to put yourself out there in the world and be subjected to criticism and disappointment.

It hurts to be criticized, but letting our fear of other people's negative responses prevent us from even trying is infinitely worse. In my opinion, fear is the single greatest barrier to reaching our greatest selves. When we operate from a place of fear, we are in protection mode. We don't try things because we want to protect ourselves from failure and/or being criticized.

Here is the cruel irony. What starts out as protecting ourselves from the pain of criticism and rejection ultimately shields us from our ability to have the things that we most fear we will never have. We are afraid that critics will expose the weaknesses that might prevent us from achieving the things that matter to us, but by not trying we can never achieve them.

Although criticism and rejection do exist, the fear of them is sometimes more imagined than real.

There are two types of fear—real and imagined. An example of a situation where real fear is warranted is if you are being chased by someone who wants to harm you. Imagined fear is when you assume your boss or new friend no longer likes you. Imagined fear is when you are worried about screwing up in a game and causing your team to lose. Imagined fear is thinking you will never amount to anything or you will never find love.

The thing you fear happening hasn't happened yet, but the dreadful anticipation of it makes it feel like it already has. There is no difference biochemically in the brain between real or imagined fear.[46] And, each type of fear has the same negative result on our bodies—stress, which produces anxiety.

Imagination is a powerful thing. Researchers at the University of Colorado and the Icahn School of Medicine created a study that showed how real and imagined responses to things we dread are very similar.[47]

The scientists measured brain activity responses of research subjects to a sound that was accompanied by an uncomfortable shock. Researchers found the brain responses to those who actually heard the negative sound and those who imagined it were incredibly identical. In the brain imaging, the real and imagined fears were shown to be the same! Here is the good news. The researchers also found that we can use imagination to retrain our brains to reduce or even eliminate our fears. In the study, two groups who heard or imagined the negative sound had their fear extinguished when the sound stopped being accompanied by a shock.[48]

So is the answer to imagine that negative things won't happen and that will make them disappear? Of course not. Imagining away the fear of what might happen is not the answer. Reimagining the consequences of what happens is what sets us free. You might lose, and it might hurt, but after it happens, you realize that you will be okay.

Wow, what a thought—it's okay to fail!

Thomas Edison failed one thousand times before inventing the first practical incandescent light bulb in 1879. He simply said, "The lightbulb was an invention with one thousand steps."

Remember, failure is being one step closer to your best self.

We want many things, but at the top is to be loved and to be accepted for who we are. We want to feel good about ourselves and to feel like we have accomplished something in life. We want to make something of ourselves and be a real contributor to our family, and ultimately, to society. Unfortunately, to have these good feelings, we must take personal risks by putting ourselves out there in the world. We must be willing to be more open and create a vulnerability from within, which may subject us to criticism and disappointment.

It takes courage to try new things, to be vulnerable with ourselves and others. It's an awful feeling that you're not good enough or someone doesn't like you, especially if you like them. That's all right because the important thing is being you and not being afraid to express yourself. You don't have to be perfect or be someone you're not. And, you don't have to be right all the time. This fear of criticism and disappointment will prevent you from creating the life you want, so you must overcome it. Be vulnerable, and you will go a long way towards doing so.

Know that you cannot have real love if you don't open up to another and be transparent. The risk is rejection. You can't have real success in the classroom without asking questions. The risk is looking stupid. You can't have real accomplishment on the court without stepping on it to play. The risk is you lose or worse, you embarrass yourself, and your peers ridicule you.

Don't be afraid to be vulnerable! Take off the mask, put yourself out there and be willing to be you, knowing that being you is good enough. I know one thing; you will be more positive, more at peace, and a happier person if you choose this path.

It is time for you to step into your own uncharted waters. To let go of your fears. To start dreaming again. To start believing again because your thoughts ultimately become your reality, your world.

Athletes know they can always perform their best when they are in a relaxed state, also known as "the zone." It's virtually impossible to be in fear mode and the zone simultaneously. If you fear making a mistake, trust me, you will not perform to your true capability. So, embrace each moment because fear doesn't live there!

Have the courage to move through your fears and take risks, knowing you may fail. But know, in taking these steps, you are moving closer to your ultimate destiny—just like Coco and her magical run through Wimbledon. Imagine if fear had stopped her and the inspiration that she provided? Don't let fear stop your magic from happening too.

As you begin to consider how to take the necessary steps to move past fear, a great place to start is seemingly so obvious that it might surprise you—remember to breathe.

BREATHE

IT WAS A TYPICAL HOT AND HUMID late August evening in Austin, Texas, as one hundred thousand people filed into Texas Memorial Stadium to watch the hometown University of Texas Longhorns football team open up the 2013 season. Most everyone in attendance anticipated a blowout over the lightly regarded visiting Aggies from New Mexico State.

I was at the game with Allyson and our family, because the Aggies starting quarterback on that evening was our son, Andrew. This was his very first start in D-1 college football. Can you imagine how nervous he must have been? And can you imagine how nervous his parents and family were? We were probably more nervous!

Andrew took a circuitous route to his special moment. As a high school football player, it was Andrew's dream to play in the Pac-10, and he originally walked on at Arizona. Andrew possessed great confidence, something he acquired through the sheer grit of overcoming many obstacles in his life.

Let's start with Andrew's birthday—July 31. That wouldn't be a big deal except for the fact that it was the cutoff date for his youth sports league, and he was always playing catch-up as the youngest player on all of his teams. To make matters worse, he was a late bloomer, meaning he matured later in life, making him undersized relative to his competitors and teammates.

Andrew also had to overcome some injuries in high school and as a freshman in college. His injuries and lack of opportunities to get beyond the scout team at Arizona frustrated Andrew, and when self-doubt started to creep in, he made some poor decisions. It soon became clear to Andrew that he had begun to lose his way and that the Pac-10 wasn't the right fit.

Andrew had to find another dream, so he came home.

It is a very difficult thing to realize that this thing you have dreamed of your entire life has slipped from your grasp and is not happening. At times like this, disillusionment can grow and, if not checked, a downward spiral can occur. I know. I've been there. When my own unhappiness turned to too much drinking and time spent away from my family, I had to make a decision to change.

This desire to be better led me to take a trip to the desert for a quiet weekend of self-reflection and personal analysis. Taking the time to do that helped me immensely, so when I saw that Andrew had lost the spirit that made him so special, I suggested that we do the same. Andrew resisted. His arm was in a sling from breaking it recently, and he didn't want to go. We went regardless.

Although he would have preferred to stay home, I think Andrew would agree that those days in the desert were some of the most meaningful moments in our relationship. The weekend was a time for Andrew to get centered. He needed to get back in touch with who he was, what was important to him, what was blocking him, who he wanted to be, and why he was here.

I had recently taught a class at USC titled Life 101, a curriculum designed for self-discovery. I took Andrew through the basic components of the class. We meditated. He journaled. And we spent time just breathing. We literally worked on breathing through his frustrations, his disappointments, and his anxieties.

Life is breath!

When we stop breathing, we no longer take in oxygen that allows us to exist. The issue is we forget how to breathe, and even worse, we hold it when we get upset, angry, or tense. The simple act of initiating a deep breath slowly through the nose, then holding it for a moment before slowly releasing this breath through the mouth can stop time and relax us no matter how seemingly dire or tense the situation we are facing.

This simple act centers us and returns us to who each of us is—an empowered, all-things-are-possible being! This is an amazing technique for athletes before and during competition, or a business executive prior to an important meeting, or a student before taking a test. It releases the tension allowing for much better performance. When we are mindful of taking a correct deep breath, we are re-gifting ourselves with life.

When we returned from our trip, things started to fall in place for Andrew.

One of the first things that Andrew had to do was accept that playing in the Pac-10 was something that didn't work out.

That is life. Not everything we plan for comes true. However, accepting the need to change plans does not mean the need to stop dreaming. Keep dreaming! Andrew was determined to get back on track and, if it meant not playing in the Pac-10, it didn't mean he couldn't still play quarterback for a D-1 college.

Every dream includes a series of steps, and Andrew selected Santa Ana Community College as the next step in his journey to return to D-1 football. He killed it that 2010 season, throwing for twenty-eight touchdowns with a 69 percent completion rate on his way to All-State and All-American honors. He had schools lined up with scholarship offers, but he had to stay another season at Santa Ana before getting a full-ride scholarship to New Mexico State due to a technicality.

During his last year of eligibility, he earned his chance to be the guy, and this was not something I was going to miss! This brings us back to the sweltering day in Austin.

Andrew jogged onto the Texas Memorial Stadium field to take his first snap as the starter for a D-1 school. His dream had arrived, complete with the roar of one hundred thousand fans. What a moment! But, let's be real, this was a road game. Those Texas fans were roaring for the defense to smother him!

What was the first thing Andrew did? He took a breath.

It relaxed him in an extraordinarily challenging situation in an extremely hostile environment against a legit national powerhouse. The result was a stellar performance. Andrew completed his first nineteen pass attempts, including one touchdown in the first half! Unfortunately, the Aggies ultimately lost the game, as expected. After the final seconds ticked off the clock, the first person to come over and shake

Andrew's hand was Mack Brown, head coach of the Texas Longhorns. He said, "Did you realize you completed your first nineteen passes in the first half?"

"No, I didn't," Andrew said.

Brown continued, "You played a great game, young man." High praise from one of the great college football coaches in the long history of the game.

Life is going to throw you many challenges. There will be times when those moments threaten to get the best of you, causing stress, and forcing you to underperform. Breathe! They call it choking for a reason. Breathe! Breath can become constricted when the pressure turns up, and you forget to breathe. Don't forget the simple, yet powerful, act of taking a deep breath.

For those of you who want to take it a step further, there are numerous apps and YouTube videos that can put you through a simple meditative breathing exercise. Breathe!

Although breathing, meditating, and reflecting can do wonders to get you through challenging times, it is also important to understand that none of us can get through life completely on our own. It is not only okay but advisable to ask others for help. There is no greater sign of strength and courage than the act of doing this.

MENTAL ILLNESS

KEVIN LOVE WAS BORN to be a basketball player.

The son of former NBA player Stan Love, Kevin Love has been a top performer on the world's largest basketball stages. He was an All-American and Pac-12 Player of the Year as a freshman at UCLA, where he led the Bruins to the Final Four. Selected fifth overall in the NBA draft, Love has made the All-Star team five times, was the league rebounding leader in 2011, and won a championship with the Cleveland Cavaliers in 2016. He also won gold medals representing the United States at the 2010 World Championships in Turkey and the 2012 Olympics in London.[49]

Although Love has enjoyed a stellar career, it has also been marred by various injuries, including broken hands, a dislocated shoulder, several concussions, and surgery to remove loose cartilage from the knee. However, he didn't think he had a heart problem until one crazy night when he was rushed from a game to the hospital.

It was an early-season game in November of 2017 when Love's Cleveland Cavaliers were hosting the Atlanta Hawks, and right from the start of the game, he didn't feel well. Things got progressively worse, and in the second half, he ran off the court and into the locker room, where he collapsed on the floor. Lying on the ground and having a hard time breathing, Love thought he was having a heart attack. In an essay that Love wrote for The Players' Tribune, he said, "I was just hoping my heart would stop racing. It was like my body was trying to say to me, *You're about to die.*" A member of the Cavaliers organization accompanied Love to the Cleveland Clinic, where they ran a series of tests, and he was relieved to learn that his heart was just fine.[50]

Love had suffered a panic attack.

Two days later, Love was back in the line-up in a game against the Milwaukee Bucks. He scored thirty-two points in a Cavaliers win, but something still didn't feel right. Although he felt good about being back in action, he recalled feeling relieved that not many people knew why he left the game against the Hawks. Love wrote in *The Players' Tribune* , "I'd thought the hardest part was over after I had the panic attack. It was the opposite. Now I was left wondering why it happened—and why I didn't want to talk about it."[51]

Love didn't want to be perceived as soft by his teammates and other players in the league. Ironically, a player who had proven his grit time after time when fighting back from numerous physical injuries was now concerned that admitting a mental health challenge might make people question his toughness. "I'd never heard of any pro athlete talking about mental health, and I didn't want to be the only one. I didn't want to look weak."[52]

The other thing that made Love reluctant to seek help was the idea that when faced with challenges in your life, you are supposed to dig in and figure it out for yourself. Men should be strong and not talk about their feelings. Fortunately for him, Love overcame his reluctance to seek help, and he began to see a therapist. He quickly learned that just talking to someone unveiled issues buried for a long time and that understanding those issues made them more manageable to deal with.

As Love saw what seeking help did for him, he also began to realize he was not the only one. A turning point came when he read DeMar DeRozan's comments about struggling with mental health. An eleven-year star in the NBA, DeRozan told the *Toronto Star* that he had dealt with depression since childhood and had recently sunk into a bout with the blues during the NBA All-Star weekend.[53]

Seeing another player speak up emboldened Love to write the essay for *The Players' Tribune.* He felt it was time to take a stand. He wanted to let people know that everyone struggles with challenges in their life and that when those challenges become too large to handle on your own, the best thing to do is seek help.

In an interview with Jason Rosario on his show "Dear Men," Love explained how his article inspired other players in the league to approach him. He said, "I've had a number of guys that actually haven't expressed themselves at all publicly but have come up to me and asked, 'How can I get help?'"[54]

Both Love and DeRozan have emerged as leaders in the NBA on the issue of mental health. Love is rightly proud of his work in eliminating the stigma that the issue carries with it. He told Rosario, "Being vulnerable is very important. I think that's another word that has a negative connotation to it; especially when it comes to masculinity and manlihood, you feel like you can't be vulnerable." Love added, "I think it's important we have these conversations."[55]

If we define illness as an unhealthy condition of the body or mind, then it is probably safe to say everyone to some degree has experienced some form of mental illness in their lifetime. It could be as simple as being a little bit off or not feeling like your normal self. Maybe you are clouded with doubts about your life, or you're anxious about what lies ahead, causing your heart to race a bit or finding it difficult to breathe normally.

These episodes can be short-lived or chronic. If they are one-off kinds of experiences, there are techniques that we've discussed in this book to calm yourself, such as having a sense of gratitude, practicing meditation, or breathing techniques. However, if the level and frequency of your condition are more problematic, it would serve you well to seek professional medical assistance that can help you move through them.

A major issue with mental illness in our world is how to create a greater culture of transparency and mainstream acceptance to discuss the challenges we have openly. It's gotten better, but just as Kevin Love's story reveals, the reluctance to acknowledge these challenges can still sometimes prohibit us from talking about them.

If someone's body breaks down, the public generally doesn't have a problem accepting the issue because it's a body they can see. But the mind cannot be seen, which casts doubt on the reality and severity of those experiencing the mental illness or "dis-ease." This makes sense, though, because society mostly operates from a "seeing is believing" mindset instead of a "believing is seeing" one.

This is where acceptance comes in. The fact that an illness manifested in someone's body doesn't mean they are different or weak. It simply means they have a health issue that must be addressed. It is time to start embracing those who have the courage to be vulnerable by coming forward to remove the stigma surrounding mental illness.

For those of you who have the courage to talk about your challenges with mental illness, you are a hero because talking about it could very likely save the life of someone who sought help when they heard you and no longer felt alone. There is nothing more heroic than saving someone's life, and so people like Kevin Love and DeMar DeRozan are to be saluted and honored for their courage and willingness to reveal their own pain to help others.

My brother, Chris, was one of these people.

I recall going with Chris to see *A Beautiful Mind*, a movie about mathematician John Nash, a Nobel Prize winner for Economics who suffered from paranoid schizophrenia. The great struggles that Nash endured in his life were masterfully portrayed by Russell Crowe. As we walked out of the theater, Chris turned to me and said, "Now you know what my life is like."

Wow! I knew my brother had some mental issues. I knew he was on some hardcore psych medications. I also knew he bounced around several high schools and colleges when he was younger, but seeing the film gave me a much greater appreciation of what was really going on inside his head. It wasn't good. As you may recall, in the movie, Nash heard voices and had vivid hallucinations where he believed people were out to get him. He was a tormented soul who learned to deal with his visions without drugs and with help from his incredible wife.

Even though my mom was a caregiver extraordinaire, my brother wasn't so fortunate. At one point, he was on so many drugs that my mother had to write them down on a five-by-seven-inch index card. She used the entire space of the card to show other doctors all of Chris's medications when he had appointments for his physical body to avoid adverse interactions for anything they might be prescribing. These drugs led to side effects requiring other drugs with other side effects. It was awful to see Chris endure all of his challenges.

I learned a lot from Chris.

Through his weight gain, weight loss, and horrible thoughts that periodically raced through his mind, Chris never complained. He was my biggest fan and supporter. He was always there to help me by running routes to keep my arm in shape when I was home visiting before summer training camp. He thought of others before himself.

Chris had compassion for others who struggled because he struggled. He was gentle and had a certain childlike innocence when most people would probably be raging. He always thought of others and brought a smile to every occasion.

Chris passed away on October 24, 2010, at the age of fifty-seven. He didn't win a Nobel Prize, but he did positively impact everyone he came in contact with. He impacted me in profound ways. He taught me to have gratitude for the smallest and simplest pleasures; from Chris, I learned that loving and serving are the greatest things we can do.

VII. FORGIVE

Let go of all failures and mistakes—
forgive yourself and others

FORGIVE YOURSELF

"I'VE BEEN SICK TO MY STOMACH for playing this final, so maybe I was not ready to win it. But hopefully I can play another final in the future, and win it."[56]

These were the words of Simona Halep at center court after losing in the 2017 French Open final. It was an especially heartbreaking defeat because she had won the first set and was up 3–0 in the second set, three games from her first Grand Slam championship. Then she fell apart, losing the match and the title, 4–6, 6–4, 6–3.

It never seemed that Halep would be able to win her battle with nerves and secure a major championship. Still, two years later, at the 2019 Wimbledon tournament, she obliterated the field, including Serena Williams in the final, 6–2, 6–2, and Halep won the championship.

Halep has emerged as one of the great stars of women's tennis, but it has been a rollercoaster ride to the top. In 2014, at the age of twenty-two, Halep had already won several tournaments and made it to the French Open final. Her trajectory was rising, but then in 2015 and 2016, she hit a wall.

The biggest issue that Halep faced was overcoming her natural predisposition to be negative. To put it simply, she beat herself up too much when things went wrong. As a result, watching a Halep match was akin to a Shakespearian drama. She stormed through matches, screaming at the skies, tossing her racquet, and kicking at the ground after missing shots.

In 2016, Halep hired Darren Cahill as her coach. There were certainly many strategic and technical things that he helped her with, but probably the most important was his insistence she also work on her mental approach to the game. In a *New Yorker* article about Halep, Cahill said, "She became her worst enemy quite often."[57]

It got so bad that Cahill temporarily left her. It's not supposed to work that way. In professional tennis, a coach is hired and fired by the player, but in a twist, Cahill fired Halep because he felt that she wasn't working hard enough to improve her mindset. It all came to a boiling point at the 2017 Miami Open.

The *New Yorker* article told how Cahill was called over by Halep between the second and third set of a quarterfinal match against Johanna Konta. Halep had won the first set and was two points from victory when her game started to unravel, and she lost the second set. Cahill tried to encourage her, but Halep replied, "I'm so bad. I'm ridiculous bad." When asked how she could correct her errors, Halep just stared at the ground with no response.[58]

Halep lost the third set and the match. After the match, Cahill told Halep he was done coaching her. Halep realized that to get him back, and more importantly, to get her career back on the right track, she would need to heed his words. Halep told *Tennis.com* she was shocked to lose her coach. She explained that he had nothing to complain about when it came to her work ethic, but she needed to change her negative mindset for him to return. Halep added that she worked hard and did make changes to her attitude.[59]

Focusing on having a more positive mindset brought Halep quick dividends. She reached the semi-final at the Stuttgart Open, won the Madrid Open, and reached the final at the Rome Open. After the Stuttgart tournament, Halep told *Tennis.com* that she asked Cahill to return. "He said yes, because I improved a lot, and he saw that I really wanted to change."[60]

After Rome, Halep marched through the field at the French Open and, once again, reached the final. Although she acknowledged that nerves had gotten the best of her, and she lost, Halep's mindset slowly improved. In the aftermath of losing a Grand Slam championship that was within her grasp, Halep was understandably down, but she began to realize that when things didn't go her way, the best response is to forgive herself and keep striving to get better. As she told *The New Yorker*, the priority was to first grow as "a person, not a tennis player."[61]

Halep worked with psychologist Alexis Castorri to redirect her energy away from the negative outbursts that were her trademark on the court. *The New Yorker* article stated, "She and Castorri worked on visualizing how she would conduct herself on the court. She chose words of encouragement to focus on in times of stress. She started to explore why it was that she was so hard on herself."[62]

Although Halep readily acknowledged that she would continue having a hard time overcoming disappointing defeats, a series of press conferences at the 2018 Indian Wells tournament showed that she had come to grasp a new approach. Halep told the reporters, "I'm always looking for perfection, but at the same time, I know that doesn't exist."[63] She later said, "So now I'm trying to change that, to be kinder with myself."[64]

Less than three months after that Indian Wells tournament, Halep finally had her Grand Slam breakthrough. In the French Open final, she faced Sloane Stephens, the defending US Open champion. The ability to bounce back from adversity was mightily tested in this match. Stephens took the first set 6–3 and was up 2–0 in the second set. Unlike in Miami, Halep did not crumble under self-doubt. She came roaring back to win 3–6, 6–4, 6–1.[65]

A year later, Halep's amazing run through the field at Wimbledon culminated with her second Grand Slam championship trophy. An amazing achievement. However, it was a few months earlier, in her interview with *The New Yorker,* that really showed how far Halep had come. She said, "My focus is not on the result. It's growing up as a person." Halep added, "A process. A big picture."[66]

Everyone makes mistakes! It could be a lousy play in a big moment of a game that caused the defeat. It could be something you said to a loved one or a friend that you wish you could take back because the relationship never recovered. It could be a poor career decision you made that caused you to tread water instead of elevating you to C-Suite status. It could be a bad investment, which set you back financially for years. It could be aligning with a group of friends that put you in the wrong place at the wrong time and landed you into deep trouble. It could be any promise you made to yourself that you continue to break.

We are often our own worst enemy, unable to forgive ourselves for mistakes that we have made. For many of us, this inability to be kind to ourselves and let go of our past failings is the single biggest obstacle that we must overcome. Often, it will take something dramatic to happen to get your attention, like a coach firing you—as in Simona Halep's case!

It doesn't matter what the regret may be. What matters is where do you go from here? Do you continually live in the past and dwell on an error in judgment or a mistake made that negatively impacted you? If you could only go back to reset history, unfortunately, that isn't possible in this dimension. If you continue to hold onto a past that you wish could be changed, then you will never realize your true potential—the one that lies ahead.

The only solution to this living hell is to let go and forgive yourself for being human. When you truly let go, you will be able to feel a weight lifted from your being. You will be lighter, and you will have created space for other amazing experiences to gravitate to you! Here's more good news: once you forgive yourself for past mistakes, you will be better able to forgive others for any harm directed your way.

You are human, and you've made mistakes, but you can take control by moving on with your life. Living in the past is the surest way to not have peace in the present. And, without peace in this moment, the future that you believe you want is clouded. When you free yourself from past screwups, the time becomes ripe to plan for a clearer and more achievable road ahead.

As you let go of the mistakes you've made that are holding you back, it is also important to not let transgressions others have made against you fester and create stress within you that hasn't been released. Forgiving yourself is incredibly important, but so is forgiving others.

FORGIVE OTHERS

WHAT WOULD YOU DO IF the single greatest moment of
your career was stolen by the mistake of another person?
Or if your greatest pain was caused by the people you loved
the most?

Venezuelan pitcher Armando Galarraga had a journey-
man Major League Baseball career with a lifetime 26–34
record and 4.78 earned run average (ERA). Although he had
an awesome 2008 rookie season with the Detroit Tigers, his
performance had dropped so dramatically by the start of the
2010 season that he was sent back to the minor leagues.

In May of 2010, Galarraga was called back up by the
Tigers and put in the starting rotation. He won his first start
but lost the next two and had a mediocre 4.50 ERA going into
a home game on June 2 against the Cleveland Indians.[67] And
then magic.

Going into the ninth inning of that game, Galarraga had
faced twenty-four batters and recorded twenty-four outs. He
was three outs away from being only the twenty-first pitcher

in all of MLB history to throw a perfect game. The Indians first batter, Mark Grudzielanek, hit a rope heading for the outfield wall, but Tigers centerfielder Austin Jackson made a running over-the-shoulder catch to keep the perfect game alive. The next Indians batter grounded out. One out away. The hometown Tigers fans rose to their feet and cheered, ready to witness history. No such luck.[68]

The Indians' Jason Donald hit a slow roller to the right of Tigers first baseman, Miguel Cabrera, which forced him off the bag to make the play. As Donald raced down the line, Galarraga was forced to cover and received a soft toss from Cabrera as he neared first base. Galarraga and Donald both arrived at the bag at about the same time. The first base umpire, Jim Joyce, made a loud and sure call. Safe!

The howls of protest from the Tigers dugout put a pit in Joyce's stomach. Joyce later told ESPN that he knew from their reaction that he might have missed the call. Galarraga retired the next batter and ended the game with a one-hitter. After the game, Joyce and the rest of the umpire crew rushed off the field to the boos of the crowd. As he entered the umpires' dressing room, Joyce immediately asked to be shown a replay of the play. What he saw drove him to tears. He had blown the call and cost Galarraga a spot in the history books.[69]

What happened next is as good an example of honor, class, and respect that you will ever see in sports.

The umpires' room at major league ballparks is typically off-limits to the media, but after seeing he had missed the call, Joyce called in reporters to set the record straight and acknowledge his mistake. Joyce tearfully told the media he took a perfect game away "from that kid over there."[70]

After the media left the umpires' room, the Tigers general manager Dave Dombrowski and manager Jim Leyland came to visit Joyce. They both knew that Joyce, a stand-up guy who was easily considered one of the best umpires in the game, would be gutted by the call. Over a post-game beer, they consoled Joyce and told him that he would need to move on past his mistake.

Joyce asked them if he could visit with Galarraga. A few moments later, when Galarraga entered the room, Joyce tearfully apologized to him. Galarraga's very simple but profound response was to hug Joyce and tell him, "We are all human."[71]

Galarraga's reaction was meant to relieve Joyce from the burden of feeling bad for his mistake. However, I would argue that an even bigger burden had been lifted from Galarraga himself. He refused to carry the baggage of "what could have been" for the rest of his life. He refused to play the victim card.

How many times do you hear people complain that they did not get the promotion they deserved because the boss didn't like them or another employee had gamed the system? How many kids (and their parents) complain that they did not make the team because the coach was playing politics? They might say the other kid's parents donated more to the booster club or the other kid played on a club team that the coach was paid to lead.

How often do you hear people gripe that their team lost because the refs were horrible? This is especially prevalent in youth sports (although the quality of officiating is sometimes

not great in youth games, especially if the refs are volunteers).
It's a convenient excuse, but I can assure you that the vast,
vast, vast majority of games are lost because the other team
played better. Period.

Even in situations like Galarraga's, where it is obvious that
someone else's actions harmed you, the inability to let go of
those transgressions can cause huge damage to your future
performance and can often carry the potential to create a
lifetime of unhappiness and even poor health.

It's one thing when the sin is related to a game or a job,
but what do you do when the harm is much greater, and the
person causing the pain is someone close to you, maybe even
your parents?

As an adult, James Jones played nine seasons in the NFL,
where he won a title with the Green Bay Packers in the 2011
Super Bowl. In 2012, he led the NFL in most touchdown
grabs with fourteen, and, in 2014, he led the Oakland Raiders
with the most receptions with seventy-three and touchdown
catches with six.[72] The dude put up great numbers throughout
his career.

As a child, Jones held a different type of statistic. He was
one of the estimated two hundred thousand to five hundred
thousand people in America who were homeless during the
1990s. Jones and his mother spent many evenings in homeless
shelters, motel rooms, and even sleeping on park benches.

Jones's mother struggled with drug addiction, as did his
father, who had left them after the couple divorced when
Jones was only eighteen months old. With his father out of the
picture, Jones stayed by his mother's side during some pretty

bleak times. In an interview with ESPN's Michelle Beisner, he recounted one of the lowest moments when he had to resort to begging so they could eat. Jones told Beisner, "My mom hadn't ate in probably two or three days, so I went into a pizza parlor and I told the guy, 'Can I just have a pizza? I promise you, man, I'll pay you back.' And I stood in that pizza parlor for probably over an hour begging this man, and he finally gave me a pizza and I took it to my mom."[73]

At the age of fifteen, Jones finally found some stability when he moved into his grandmother's house, and he began to excel at football. Even though he no longer lived with his mother, she did not abandon him, attending all of his games (and later, she was able to achieve sobriety).

Jones always forgave his mother for the pain her addiction inflicted on his childhood. In an interview for the San Diego Chargers website he explained his decision to move in with his grandmother. "My mom was doing very badly. I kind of felt like I was a little bit of extra luggage for her (and that) she would be better on her own, trying to get back on her feet. I was just a kid. I couldn't help her and didn't have the sense to (tell her) she needed to stop doing drugs. I told my mom, 'You need to get on your feet, and it'll be easier if I'm not there.'" He later added, "My mom will tell you to this day, I never complained. I never really got down on myself because I truly never wanted my mom to feel worse than she already felt."[74]

It's natural to wonder how Jones could forgive his mother after all the hardships her addiction caused him. However, it's important to understand that people who cannot let go of previous hurts often have a challenging time appreciating all the great things that happen in their lives. The hurt blots out the joy and, until they let go, the pain always wins.

However, people who have the ability to forgive and show empathy for those who let them down are far more likely to be able to experience greater joy in their accomplishments. A perfect example for Jones of sharing that joy with his mother was when signing his first big NFL contract allowed him to make good on a childhood promise to buy her a house one day.

Carrying hurts forward not only harms our relationships with the people we cannot forgive. It also makes it very difficult to have meaningful relationships with the people that come after. The resentment and bitterness that you cannot release may not appear at first. Yet, when the inevitable disagreements that come in every relationship do surface, the inability to forgive or be forgiven can cause irreparable damage to the bond between two people.

So, how do we forgive? The first step is to be aware that you will be healthier and happier if you make a conscious effort to forgive and not hold grudges. Realize that it can sometimes be hard and so be fair to yourself. You can't really forgive others if you don't forgive yourself. Acknowledge the pain that you felt and work on releasing the emotions. This can be done by talking to others and consider getting professional help if it is required.

Have compassion. If you understand what the person who hurt you was going through or the stage of life they were in when they caused you harm, you will find it much easier to forgive them. Jones offers a great example of this. He understood that the inability of his parents to give him the care that a child deserves was rooted in the disease of addiction.

Forgiving is not forgetting. It is a choice to look for a better path forward instead of holding on to the injustices of the past. For many people who choose to forgive, that choice also comes with the understanding that letting go of the past does not mean carrying those transgressions made against them into the future in their relationships with others. Just because you were harmed does not give you a license to hurt others.

Just like many other children who were able to forgive their parents and turn the page to become much better parents to their own kids, Jones is passionate about being a great dad. He is dedicated to raising his two sons to be responsible and caring members of society. Knowing the pain of being homeless and hungry, Jones has made it a point to support shelters and serve food. When he does this, he often brings his wife and two boys to help.

The mistake that Jones's parents made to start using drugs is not unique. Unfortunately, addiction is at near epidemic levels in many places throughout the world. One of the surest strategies to avoid getting caught in that trap is to pay attention to the seemingly little things in life that can snowball into bigger issues if you are not being conscious.

VIII. BE CONSCIOUS

Stay present and be mindful of all you think, say, and do

PAY ATTENTION

BRETT FAVRE SAT in his New Orleans hotel room on the day of the Super Bowl, and he kept seeing the same highlight over and over again from the last time the game was played in the Louisiana Superdome. In the highlight, Joe Montana, the San Francisco 49ers quarterback in that game, stepped up to the line of scrimmage and looked out over the Denver Broncos defense. Montana saw them lined up in a blitz formation and started calling out an audible, "59 Razor." The play resulted in a thirty-eight-yard touchdown pass to Jerry Rice as the 49ers went on to demolish the Broncos 55–10.[75]

Later that day, Favre and his Green Bay Packers teammates stepped onto the same Superdome turf to square up against the New England Patriots in Super Bowl XXXI. As the Packers offense prepared to go out for their first series of the game, Favre huddled with his head coach, Mike Holmgren. Holmgren instructed his quarterback to start the game by just running the plays he called, nothing fancy, and no audibles until the offense got into a groove.

On the second play of the series, Favre stepped up to the line and couldn't believe his eyes. He saw that the Patriots were lined up in a blitz formation, the same defense that prompted Montana to call the Razor audible against the Broncos. Adding to Favre's surprise was the fact that Patriots defensive coordinator Bill Belichick was pretty well known in the league for strictly sticking to a zone coverage and rarely blitzing.

In typical Favre fashion, he disregarded the head coach's order, paying more attention to the defensive alignment in front of him and the unique opportunity he might have. The audible play call resulted in a fifty-four-yard touchdown pass to Andre Rison, which set the tone for a Packers 35–21 Super Bowl victory. It was a brilliant move by the Hall of Fame quarterback because he was conscious and not operating in default mode.[76]

I can't emphasize enough the need to pay attention to the things that come in front of you as you move along your path in life and to be flexible on how to deal with them when they appear.

Having a plan is keenly important, but you must be aware and capable of measuring how it's working. If things are not happening the way you envisioned, keep moving forward, and tweak some things as needed. If you continue to receive messages that you are not on the right path, then maybe you need to let go and pursue other options. More than likely, if you do let go, new options will find you.

My middle son, Andrew, is a perfect example of this need to be open-minded about changing direction.

I refer to Andrew as a foxhole guy. He is someone you can count on to show up to support and protect his friends and family when things get messy. Andrew is smart, and he's also tough and resilient because of what he's experienced and overcome in his life. His grandfather, Roger, Allyson's dad, used the term "bulletproof" to describe Andrew when he was young. He earned the nickname.

Andrew always dreamed of playing football in the Pac-10 (now Pac-12). As I've said, he was physically a late bloomer, but he was confident in his abilities to reach that goal, and we encouraged his dream. So, after a very good high school football career as a two-year starting quarterback at Newport Harbor High, Andrew was invited to become a preferred walk-on at the University of Arizona.

Although it was exciting to be on a Pac-10 team, it was not an ideal situation. To have a clear picture of the scenario that Andrew was stepping into, you have to understand that the difference between being a player on scholarship and a walk-on is like night and day in many college football programs. Walk-ons typically have minimum respect from the coaches and the players that are getting their college tuitions paid by the school. The scholarship players are the chosen few. The walk-ons are the afterthoughts.

At most schools, walk-ons are not allowed to eat at the training table with the team unless their parents paid for it. Food is not included as it is for those on scholarship. Effectively nothing is included for a walk-on, except the right to put on a uniform at practice.

On the field, the walk-ons are part of the scout team that

replicates the plays of the team's opponents. The scout team is there to make sure the team is ready for the upcoming game. In fact, if the quarterback on the scout team makes a good play, it's bad for the team's defense, and the coach will no doubt run the same play again until they get it right. If the defense makes a great play, and it includes roughing up the scout team quarterback, all the better for the team.

Effectively, scout team players are punching bags and receive virtually no love from the players and coaches. Oftentimes, members of the scout team don't feel part of the team at all. They are on the outside looking in even though they show up for every meeting, practice, and game that is required of the scholarship players.

This role as a scout team quarterback became very frustrating for Andrew, and self-doubt began to creep in. This frustration began to manifest in negative ways off the field. The University of Arizona was a noted party school, and Andrew escaped from his football challenges by drinking and partying too much. Sound familiar?

Andrew had a series of incidents where he was cited by police officers, and he even broke his right arm in a freak accident over spring break. The culmination of this downward spiral resulted in him sitting in his dorm room hungover early one morning, pondering his life and where he was headed. Andrew realized it was almost like self-sabotage because he knew he wasn't in the right place even though academically he was doing great.

Allyson and I received a call that next morning where Andrew explained what he was going through. He told us he wanted to leave Arizona and come home. So he did. He left the Pac-10 school of his dreams because life wasn't working for him. It was time for a fresh start.

Andrew was paying attention.

There is a sentiment in society that if you keep running into the same brick wall, ultimately, it will fall, or you will blast a hole through the center. This approach incurs a lot of stress on the mind and body. A better tact is to figure out how to climb over the wall or move around it, which requires thinking outside the box and being conscious.

It is certainly the appropriate response to face adversity by fighting hard and not giving up. Grit and resilience play a big factor in people's success. However, successful people also understand that the best way to respond to life's failures is to evaluate and learn from them. Sometimes this evaluation calls for a change in direction and a renewed commitment to working hard to make that new path the one that leads to success.

Andrew returned home and went back to work at a program that was a better fit for him. It wasn't the Pac-10; it wasn't even the NCAA. He got an opportunity at Santa Ana College and worked his butt off to become the starting quarterback. The dividends it paid off were awesome. Andrew accounted for sixty-five touchdowns, both passing and running, over a two-year span. He was named to the Junior College All-American team, which landed him a scholarship at New Mexico State, a D-1 NCAA football school.

At New Mexico State, Andrew became the starting quarterback in his senior year. He threw fifteen touchdown passes for the Aggies, with the opportunity to compete against major college football teams, such as the Texas Longhorns, Minnesota Golden Gophers, and UCLA Bruins. And, as I mentioned, most importantly he met Elise, the young lady he married a few years later!

Many stubbornly stick to what they know without seeking new ways. The habit is the issue! We walk through life on autopilot doing the same things we have always done even though our life isn't working. As Einstein reportedly said, but it warrants repeating: "Insanity is doing the same thing over and over and expecting different results."[77]

Why do we do keep living the same? We do so because it is what we know. It is what's comfortable. It is the known, and things could be worse. So, we don't pay attention to the repeated signs that we are off track. Trust me; these signs will continue to surface in one form or another until we open our eyes and change. If not, we will undoubtedly grow into a glazed-over zombie going through life unhappy and wake up one day wondering what happened!

Pay attention and be conscious of what you are experiencing in your life. Know that calling an audible and changing your play may be exactly what you must do to truly live the dream life that you visualize for yourself.

VISUALIZE

"IT'S JUST CRAZY what the mind can do."[78]

That's what USA National Team soccer player Carli Lloyd told George Stephanopoulos of *Good Morning America* to describe the circumstances of her hat trick against Japan in the 2015 Women's World Cup final. There is no bigger stage in soccer than a World Cup. At the 2015 championship match, Lloyd walked out onto the pitch for the start of the game with her teammates and their Japanese opponents.

Within sixteen minutes, Lloyd put herself into the history books.

In the third minute of the game, Megan Rapinoe hit a low cross on a corner kick that Lloyd redirected into the net with the outside of her left foot. In the fifth minute, another cross off a free kick landed in the six-yard box, with Lloyd beating the Japanese defenders to the ball and burying it into the goal.

And then the *coup de grâce*.

In the sixteenth minute of the match, Lloyd gathered the ball at the edge of the midfield circle on the American side of the centerline. She dribbled past a Japanese player. As she reached the centerline, Lloyd noticed that Japan's goalie was well off her line. Without hesitating, Lloyd drove a shot from sixty yards away and watched it sail just over the fingertips of the scrambling keeper.

The ball bounced off the inside of the post and into the net for a once-in-a-lifetime-type goal. Lloyd's spectacular third goal capped off her hat trick. Lloyd's amazing performance propelled the United States to capture the gold medal in a 5–2 victory over Japan.[79]

But here's the thing: Lloyd's goals had already been scored before the match even began.

At the post-match press conference, Lloyd described a workout she had in the period right before the World Cup. "It was just my headphones and myself at the field ... I just completely zoned out. I dreamed of, and visualized, playing in a World Cup final, and visualized scoring four goals."[80]

Okay, she only scored three.

All kidding aside, what Lloyd did was employ the practice of visualization. Visualization is creating a mental image of a future event you will be participating in and picturing what you hope to achieve. By doing this, you are already seeing the success in advance and imprinting it into your brain. Lloyd visualized seeing herself scoring goals in a World Cup final, and when she was there, in her mind's eye, the goals had already been scored.

Many people scoff at visualizations because some so-called self-help gurus have manipulated the concept to convince people all they have to do is dream it, and it will happen. It should be obvious, but I still feel obligated to mention that putting a picture on your bedroom wall of you scoring a goal in a big soccer game will not happen if you don't go out and do the necessary training to become a player with the ability to even be in the game in the first place.

However, for those that do the work and have gotten themselves to a place where they have a spot in the game, visualization can be a very powerful tool to give them a competitive advantage over the rest of the field. And, for those that are working hard to get on the field, visualization can train the brain to believe they are already there and give them a boost in achieving their dreams.

There are numerous scientific studies demonstrating that the brain registers what you imagine in exactly the same way as something that actually happened.

One of my favorite studies was from a neuroscientist named Alvaro Pascual-Leone, who brought two volunteer groups to the Harvard Medical School for a research project. The first group was instructed to do a simple five-finger piano playing exercise, and the second group was asked to hold their hands steady and only imagine playing the piano. The finding showed that the region of the motor cortex that controls the fingers had expanded in the brains of those who actually played the piano, and it also expanded in the brains of the volunteers who only imagined playing![81]

Visualization can also be a mindset. Do you imagine yourself as a powerful force? Or, do you look in the mirror and see a victim who is destined to lose? Sometimes it can be nuanced, so you have to pay attention (remember paying attention?). I have personally seen the amazing impact that a simple tweak in how you visualize yourself can have on performance.

My son Matthew is currently a quarterback at Bowling Green State University, but in his senior year of high school, he was the starter at Mission Viejo High in Orange County, California. As previously mentioned, Matt broke his wrist in his junior season, so he did not have a wide range of options available to achieve his dream of playing college football.

Matt needed to perform well in his senior year. But here's the thing: just like in life, you can't do it all alone. The good news is that Matt had one of the best high school wide receivers in all of California to throw to. Austin Osborne was a six-foot, two-inch, 190-pound stud athlete who had already been given a scholarship offer and had committed to playing at the University of Washington. The only problem was that Austin was in a slump, and his dropped passes could potentially harm Matt's chances of also getting a scholarship to play in college.

I arranged to meet Austin to see if I could offer anything that might help get him back on the track that made him one of the most prized wide receiver recruits in California. Two things immediately jumped out at me that could help explain his timid performances in recent games.

First, Austin was starting to feel the pressure of being seen as "the man" who had been given a scholarship to play ball at a major program like Washington, and he wasn't sure if he was worthy of the accolades. He didn't seem to be enjoying himself on the field, and that was manifesting itself into performances that were below his par. I reminded Austin how cool it was to be able to play a sport with all your friends and have more of your friends and family in the stands watching. Gratitude for that opportunity could make the game fun again and help take away the pressure he was feeling.

And then came the visualization question. I asked Austin if he could compare himself to any animal in the kingdom, which one would it be. He said it might be a gazelle because they were fast, and he was known for being a speedy receiver. I thought about it for a moment and then reminded him that cheetahs were also fast, but a cheetah could eat a gazelle. I told him to visualize what this new mindset would be and feel like for the upcoming game. I said, "See yourself as a cheetah attacking the ball while it was in the air."

The following week Austin was back to the form that made him such a sought-after recruit. He was still flying around the field with all the speed God gave him, but he was now doing it like a cheetah. Where he was previously getting knocked off balls by defenders, he was now aggressively snatching them out of the air. He was now eating instead of being eaten.

In that game, Austin caught five touchdown passes, which is the second-most in the entire history of Orange County high school football. His performance was the high point in Mission Viejo, defeating their rival El Toro High School 55–14, and Austin was named the Orange County Offensive Player of the Week.

The mental side of sports, and many other professions, is often the key separator between the best and the mediocre.

Carli Lloyd elaborated on this at the post-match press conference. She said, "The mental side of the game is a huge thing.... That's what it's all about. I think at the end of the day you can be physically strong, you can have all the tools out there, but if your mental state isn't good enough, you can't bring yourself to bigger and better things."[82]

Lloyd's idea of needing a strong mindset to reach the pinnacle of success is not rare among athletes who have reached such elite status. Like Lloyd did, many players interviewed after a championship will cite that having a strong mindset was key to their victory.

One way that more and more people are learning to develop a strong mindset is by incorporating a daily meditation routine into their lives.

MEDITATE

AS SHAWN GREEN STEPPED INTO the batter's box, scattered boos could be heard from throughout the Dodger Stadium crowd. After striking out, the sprinkling of boos turned into a downpour as Green slowly made his way back to the dugout. This was a scene that repeated itself numerous times in the early part of the 2002 baseball season.[83]

Green was struggling mightily as his batting average dipped down into the 230s. The fans could not forgive a guy who had signed a massive six-year, $84 million contract only two years prior. The boos were a very loud and rude reminder that Green was not earning his keep.

Green had to get back to the basics.

In 1997, Green was a member of the Toronto Blue Jays and was struggling to make his way into the everyday lineup. He grew especially frustrated when Blue Jays manager, Cito Gaston, and hitting coach, Willie Upshaw, forced him to go hit off a batting tee to improve his hitting form. [84]

In his book, *The Way of Baseball: Finding Stillness at 95 mph,* Green acknowledges that when he first began taking swings, they were fueled by anger and frustration. However, a few days into the process, things changed, and he began to enjoy it. After the first few swings, his mind would quiet, and the swings would start to feel more fluid. He began to enjoy the half-hour spent at the hitting tee every day.[85]

Five years later, and now one of the game's stars, Green responded to his slump by going back to the batting cage. In the book, Green discussed taking batting practice on a day off and staying so long that a blister formed on his hand. A few days later, the Dodgers were in Milwaukee for a game against the Brewers. In his first at-bat, Green roped a line-drive double. An inning later, he hit a three-run homer. This was followed by two more home runs and a single. He had five hits, including three home runs, with one more inning left to play.[86]

The work in the batting cage had busted Green out of his slump in a big way. When Green entered the batting cage in Toronto in 1997, and then again during his slump in 2002, he was certainly working on the mechanics of his swing, but there was something else going on, which Green felt was far more important. He was working on the mechanics of his mind.

Green described in the book his practice of hitting off the tee. He explained that his breathing became rhythmic. He would inhale as he put the ball on the tee, hold his breath as he got into his stance, and then exhale as he took his swing. What was happening here?" The repetitive rhythm of hitting a baseball off a tee began to morph into a form of meditation for Green as he emptied his mind and just let the natural flow of swinging the bat take over[87]

Most athletes can point to specific moments in their career when they just turned off their minds and got into a zone. They experienced moments when everything slowed down, and the game just flowed. That is a meditative state. This calm state of mind is what Green was able to enter into when facing the Brewers. Green wrote in his book that being so deep into the zone made him feel more like a spectator than a player in the game. He was outside of himself, watching himself play rather than willing the actions to happen. It was a calm experience where he observed himself hitting the ball.

After hitting three home runs, a double, and a single, Green described his last at-bat in the ninth inning of the Brewers game. He explained that as he stepped into the batter's box, he realized he was still in the zone and didn't need to concern himself with thinking about what he needed to do. He would simply look for a pitch he liked and take a hard swing at it. With the count one and one, a thigh-high fastball approached—home run.[88]

Green circled the bases as the Brewers fans all stood and gave him a standing ovation, rare for a visiting player. They recognized that they had just witnessed one of the greatest hitting performances in the history of baseball. Green went six-for-six with four home runs and nineteen total bases, a major league record.[89]

Although Green didn't practice meditation in a traditional manner, there is no mistaking that his method of batting practice created a meditative result, which he was able to tap into during the game. In the past, meditation was often seen as something that only granola-eating hippies would practice. However, that perception has radically changed, and athletes such as NBA MVP LeBron James, Cy Young Award winner Barry Zito, and NFL Pro Bowl quarterback Russell Wilson all have been noted as players who meditate.

We live in a chaotic world where there always seems to be something to do. And, if we're not busy, we feel compelled to fill the void of inactivity. This style of living creates a frenetic state, which can overload us to the point where we become stressed out. What everyone forgets is that we are not human doings; we are human beings, and we can get lost in the doing and forget how to just be.

Meditation is a fantastic way to quiet the mind through the clutter of life and reconnect with the universal flow, and ultimately your true self. You are transported from the baggage held from a traumatic past and the concerns and fears about an unknown future to the one place where life slows down—the present moment. According to neuroscientist Dr. Joseph Dispenza in his book, *Becoming Supernatural*, your brain waves can even line up with greater coherence during such meditative sessions.[8]

It's no wonder that we think more clearly and are able to perform much more consistently when we integrate meditation into our lives.

There is a vast array of types of meditative techniques from which to choose, including breath awareness, focus, mantra, walking, mindfulness, and guided meditations, to name a few. Do your own research and play around with some variations to see what works best for you. Stop thinking, trying hard, or willing things to happen and get into the flow of the moment for the pure joy of the experience.

The result will undoubtedly be a more relaxed and peaceful you, which also, paradoxically, can mean a more productive you.

IX. INNER PEACE

See the abundance that life offers and
have gratitude for all you receive

GRATITUDE

"THANK YOU"[90]

When fifteen-year-old Coco Gauff began her magical run through the 2019 Wimbledon, one of her tennis heroes, Venus Williams, was standing on the other side of the net in the tournament's first round. On the final rally of the match, Venus hit a shot into the net.

Game. Set. Match, Coco Gauff.

As the reality that she had just defeated her idol began to sink in, Coco put her hands on her head and began to weep. Then, she walked to the net and accepted a handshake and congratulations from Venus. *USA Today* reported that before Venus could walk back to her chair, Coco pulled her in closer to say a few additional words. Coco later revealed what she had told her idol. "Thank you for everything that you did. I wouldn't be here without you." She added, "I always wanted to tell her that."[91]

Having that type of gratitude for someone as young as Coco is rare. However, it is not surprising when you learn that the wisdom she exhibited came from going through challenges that most people her age have not yet experienced. The path to center court at Wimbledon comes with much more pressure than a typical fifteen-year-old has to face.

Coco realized that she had to stop trying to live up to the hype of being a rising tennis star and instead have gratitude for what she already had accomplished and how fortunate she was to just be out on the court having fun playing tennis. This focus on being grateful was nicely exhibited by her classy words to Venus.

Yahoo Sports reported that Coco explained her process of getting to a better place in a post she wrote for *Behind the Racquet.* "Everyone asks me how I stay calm on court and I think it's because I accepted who I am after overcoming low points in my life. Now, when I'm on court, I am just really thankful to be out there."[92]

Having gratitude for the big things and the small things in life is a powerful way of being. Why? If you tend to see and focus on those experiences you are grateful for, you will have a more positive outlook on life. You will have less stress, fear, and anger about the normal upsets presented in your lifetime. You'll be more at peace, and most likely, healthier.

If you don't believe me, ask a neuroscientist!

My good friend Dr. Glenn Fox is a neuroscientist at the University of Southern California who has dedicated his professional career to studying the science of gratitude. In an interview with PBS affiliate WHYY, Glenn said, "Grateful people tend to recover faster from trauma and injury. They tend to have better and closer personal relationships and may even have improved health overall."[93]

In the interview, Fox cited a study from Indiana University that divided people suffering from depression and other mental health issues into three groups. One group was asked to write letters of gratitude, a second group wrote reflections on their deepest feelings, and the third wrote nothing. The study revealed that the group that wrote the gratitude letters showed better mental health scores than the other two groups.[94]

Gratitude is especially effective when in a fearful or anxious state. We are constantly surrounded by fear. If you don't believe me, turn on the evening news. Additionally, advertising is structured to prey on our fear of loss. Social media utilizes this fear of being left out to move people to action. Fear is everywhere, which is why I rarely watch the news and lean toward inspirational stories for my entertainment.

Here's the cool thing—the more you recognize gratitude, the more experiences that will occur for which to be grateful. It's a cycle. The gift that keeps on giving. In Coco Gauff's case, her gratitude came from simply recognizing she was playing tennis because she loved it. For me, it was my love of football.

My dream, like many kids, was to play football at a major university and to be seen on television. After getting accepted by the principal to attend Bishop Amat High School, I felt that I had greatly improved my odds of realizing this dream. Amat was a stellar program in the competitive Angelus League, a breeding ground for high-profile college recruits.

It was a great plan, but it put a great burden on my parents. They didn't make enough money to afford the private school tuition. Imagine yourself as a parent in this situation. What would you do? How would you support your athlete child?

My parents were special people. My mom, Annie, was 100 percent Russian and had great pride in her heritage. She wanted to be a nurse when she was a child, but she couldn't handle the math. Years later, though, when my father, Frank, and then my brother, Chris, became ill, my mother was right there to care for them. She was an amazing caregiver!

Even though she only had a high school education, she didn't miss a thing. One day when she was about eighty-five years old, I called to check on her, and I asked, "How are you, Mom?" She said, "I am so frustrated!" I asked why and she said, "I'm off on balancing my checkbook." I tried to reassure her, so I asked by how much, to which she replied, "I'm off by one penny." I started laughing, and then she said, "I will get it right." She was a dog with a bone that would not let go. A couple of days later, she called me. "I found it. I balanced my checkbook." That's my mom.

My dad had a particularly challenging upbringing—an alcoholic father and brother, and a mother who made him quit high school and football to get a job to support the family. This was devastating for my dad because he loved football, which is why he was so encouraging to me throughout my career. He later received his high school diploma and an AA degree from a junior college while he worked at his job at Sears Department store. He was a hard worker and was able to support his family, but we did not have many discretionary funds beyond life's essentials.

My mom and dad would do anything for my brother and me. So, it was no surprise when my mom found a job cleaning an office building to cover the cost of my high school tuition at Bishop Amat. My dad would join my mom after he had worked a full day at his primary job. He would come home to eat dinner quickly before heading to the GTE building on San Bernardino Road in Covina to clean toilets.

I didn't appreciate the magnitude of the sacrifices they both made to allow me the opportunity to follow my dream until later in life. It was after I became a parent for the first time that I developed a profound level of respect and love for who they were as people and how much they cared and sacrificed for their family. If they had not made this decision to put their own lives on hold for me, I would not have made it to the huge stage of big-time college football or the NFL.

I had an immense sense of gratitude for their act of love and commitment to their family and to me. Would you do this for your children? What if you were the child—how much gratitude would you have for this incredible act of sacrifice and love?

A great way to remind yourself of the things you are thankful for is to keep a daily gratitude journal and jot them down. It literally could be anything that brings you peace and comfort, allowing you to move through the fear and anxiety. It could be something as simple as a beautiful sunset that activates a moment of awe, hearing your child laughing in the next room, or getting together with friends to watch a movie. As you start doing this, you will quickly learn that there is an abundance of things to be grateful for.

ABUNDANCE

THE NFL QUARTERBACK POSITION is unique in sports. It is one of the only spots where the backup typically gets absolutely no playing time, other than being inserted late into games, where the outcome has already been decided. Being a backup QB can significantly test the character of a player and especially his ability to put the good of the team ahead of his own personal interests.

Alex Smith passed this test, not once, but twice, and the strong character he exhibited was later called upon to get him through a trial that was infinitely more important than making it onto the field during a game.

Smith was the overall first pick in the 2005 NFL Draft, chosen by the San Francisco 49ers to be the quarterback of their future. It did not start out well. In his first season, Smith played in nine games, throwing for only one touchdown and eleven interceptions. In his first six seasons with the 49ers, the team had a dismal won-loss record of 37–59, and Smith's performances were inconsistent during this span.[95]

In 2011, the 49ers hired Jim Harbaugh as their head coach, and everything changed. The team finished 13–3 during the regular season and entered their first playoff game in nine years. In that game, versus the New Orleans Saints, Smith threw for 299 yards, three touchdowns, and no interceptions. In the game's last four minutes, Smith led the 49ers to two long touchdown drives, capping one with a twenty-eight-yard touchdown run and the other with a fourteen-yard touchdown pass to Vernon Davis to give San Francisco a 36–32 victory.[96]

Although the 49ers lost the 2011 NFC championship game to the New York Giants, they were on track in 2012 to make the Super Bowl. And that is exactly what they did, but Smith was on the sideline for that game, which the 49ers lost to the Baltimore Ravens, 34–31.[97]

The 49ers started the 2012 season with Smith as starting quarterback, but in the ninth game of the season, he suffered a concussion, and Colin Kaepernick replaced him. Although Smith was having the best season of his career and was the third-rated passer in the NFL, Kaepernick caught fire and kept the job.

There is an unwritten rule in sports that players who lose their starting spot because of an injury will typically get it back when they heal. Smith could have raised hell and demanded his job back. He was playing really well before he got hurt. But he didn't complain. Instead, he supported Kaepernick and the team. Coach Harbaugh would later say that Smith was a great coach to Kaepernick during that season. The coaching paid huge dividends as Kaepernick led the 49ers to their first Super Bowl in eighteen seasons.[98]

The following season Smith was traded by the 49ers to the Kansas City Chiefs. The Chiefs were coming off a terrible 2–14 season and had only made the playoffs in two of the previous nine years. Under new coach Andy Reid, and with Smith at quarterback, the Chiefs immediately turned things around, going 11–5 in their first season and making the playoffs.

Going into the 2017 season, the Chiefs had made the playoffs in three of the four years that Smith was their quarterback, and he was elected to the Pro Bowl twice. In 2016, Smith had the best season of his career, leading the Chiefs to a 12–4 record before losing to the Pittsburgh Steelers in the playoffs.[99] However, in the 2017 NFL Draft, the Chiefs chose quarterback Patrick Mahomes with their first-round pick.

The Chiefs did not select Mahomes to replace Smith for the 2017 season, but they did pick him to become their quarterback of the future. By 2017, Smith had already been in the NFL for twelve seasons, and the expiration tag on his career could easily be considered fast approaching. Smith led the Chiefs to another playoff appearance and, off the field, he took Mahomes under his wing to teach him the ropes.[100] Smith did this even though it meant that he was helping to groom the guy who would replace him, and that is what happened. Smith rejected the temptation to have a scarcity mindset.

So, what exactly is scarcity mindset?

People with a scarcity mindset tend to focus obsessively on the things they don't have, and this often leads to poor decision making, which negatively impacts their long-term success. Harvard professor of psychology Sendhil Mullainathan cowrote a book with Princeton psychology professor Eldar

Shafir where they gathered decades of scientific research to explain this theory. In *Scarcity: Why Having Too Little Means So Much*, the professors showed that excessively thinking about the things you don't have creates a self-fulfilling prophesy where your actions cause you to become exactly what you feared most. For example, if you don't have a lot of money, the obsession with being poor causes you to be trapped in a mindset that ultimately keeps you in poverty.[101]

We live in a society where we are often taught that everyone is battling for their piece of the pie, for their place or position on this planet. The belief is our world is finite, and there is only so much to go around, so you better get yours before it's gone. It's a "dog eat dog," "survival of the fittest" mindset where life is a win or lose game. This belief breeds anxiety, fear, anger, and ultimately, unhappiness.

Is this the only way to live? It's not. The opposite of a scarcity mindset is an abundance mindset.

Abundance is defined in the *Oxford Dictionary* as "a large quantity that is more than enough."[102] So, having a feeling of abundance will create a state where you are satiated or satisfied. You are probably wondering, "How do I get this feeling of abundance if I'm still hungry or I can't pay my rent?"

In order to manifest anything, you already have to possess it.

Now, what does that mean? The reason we want something—a new car, more money, a better life, is because we don't have it, right? This quote means that we must have a sense of abundance and see it around us before we receive what we want. However, the key to an abundance mindset is to be satisfied with what you have received and not obsessed with what you don't.

If you wake up in the morning and you see and appreciate a marvelous sunrise, that is abundance. If you're meeting a friend that day for coffee and he buys, that's abundance. When you pulled into the lot for coffee, and there is a parking space with time left on the meter, that is abundance. Seeing the abundance in smaller experiences can lead to a change within that creates satisfaction with what you have received. When this satisfaction grows because you are noticing more reasons to feel abundant, better things will start to happen for you.

Alex Smith's story is the textbook example of having an abundance mindset. When another quarterback on the team's roster emerged above him, he could have pouted and focused on what he no longer had. He could have obsessed with being seen as a backup, but he stayed positive and kept coming to work to support his team.

At the conclusion of the 2017 season, Smith was traded by the Chiefs to Washington. Although Kansas City did not see him as the quarterback of their future, Smith's positive attitude and refusal to have a scarcity mindset were rewarded with a massive pot of gold in Washington. The team signed Smith to a four-year $94 million contract![103]

Smith immediately proved that Washington's faith in him was warranted. In the five seasons prior to Smith's arrival, the team had a 31–48–1 record, but in his first nine games at starter, Smith led Washington to a 6–3 record with a clear path to the playoffs in front of them.[104]

And then, in Smith's tenth game, disaster struck.

The Houston Texans arrived in Washington for a matchup of two 6–3 teams. It was a tight game, with both teams competing for a playoff spot in their respective conferences. With a little under eight minutes left in the third quarter, Smith was sacked by Houston's J.J. Watt and Kareem Jackson. As Smith lay on his back with his hands covering his face, his nearest teammate immediately signaled for the team trainer to come out to the field.[105] It was clear something bad had happened as scores of players from both teams poured onto the field to wish him well while he was being carted away.[106]

Smith suffered a compound, spiral leg fracture that extended from his ankle to his knee with bone protruding through his skin. When Smith arrived at the hospital, he went straight into surgery. It was the first of Smith's seventeen surgeries, but even as bad as that number sounds, it was far from the worst of it. Infection from Smith's injury caused flesh-eating bacteria to ravage his leg, and he was not responding to the antibiotics that the doctors were giving him.

As Smith's fever spiked and his situation rapidly deteriorated, his wife, Elizabeth Smith, asked his doctors to consider amputating his leg to save his life. In *Project 11*, an ESPN *E60* documentary, Elizabeth said that she told them, "My husband is lying here and he's dying and it's coming from his leg. I just need to know, why can't we just cut it off?[107] She added, "Just make sure that he gets up, wakes up, and we get him out of here and I don't care if it's with one or no legs, we need to make sure he's okay."[108]

Fortunately, the doctors finally got Smith's infection under control and prevented amputation, but they had to remove a significant amount of infected muscle from his leg. In order to salvage his limb, they would need to surgically take muscle from other parts of his body and transplant them to his leg. Although the procedure was successful, it left him incapable of lifting up his ankle or foot.

Smith's injury was so severe that he went to be examined by military doctors that typically treat battlefield injuries. This is where Smith began his rehab. The expectation for the extent of his recovery was fairly limited. In *Project 11*, Smith explained his initial goals. "This was really about life, waking up in the middle of the night and going to the bathroom, and showering the rest of my life, and playing with my kids."[109]

At one point in his life, Smith was on top of the world. He earned a massive contract playing football in front of thousands of adoring fans and millions more on TV. However, when that was all taken away, he had the opportunity to see how important the little things are in life. As he started to heal, just taking a shower and the chance to play with his kids was something he was incredibly grateful to have again.

When we feel gratitude in seemingly minor experiences, such as the ability to shower or chase our kids around a park, our perception of reality begins to change. We will begin to focus more on what we have, not on what we do not have. And, this shift in focus sow the seeds of growth that allow us to be more positive, feel better about ourselves, and have a more fulfilled life.

Gratitude allows us to live life in a more relaxed state of mind and let things come naturally to us rather than obsessing over what we don't have. This obsession shows a lack of belief, and belief plays a massive role in living an abundant life. First, you must believe it is possible to receive abundance.

You can convince yourself it is possible by acknowledging others around you who are living such a life instead of being angry at them for being so fortunate. And, most importantly, you must believe you deserve abundance in your life. One way to believe we are worthy is to notice the smaller examples of abundance happening for us every single day.

As Smith's leg bone began healing and his rehab progressed, the strong inner drive that he always possessed began to kick in, and he started thinking about how far he might be able to push the recovery. He said, "Can I go play quarterback again? Can I push it that far? Football might not be out of the question."[110]

Although Smith wanted to give football another shot and believed it might be possible, he also never lost sight of the fact that he was fortunate to be alive and able to move about freely again. In a follow-up ESPN interview with Scott Van Pelt, Smith said, "It's all icing on the cake right now. I can play with my kids. There's so many things in life that I doubted I'd ever be able to do again and to have those behind me, it's all gravy now. But my mentality's no different, I'm chasing just as hard."[111]

Miraculously, Smith did return and made it back to the Washington squad as their quarterback. His sense of abundance, gratitude, and belief was rewarded with a chance to play on the greatest stage again. His story is an amazing reminder that we should never give up and keep going for it again and again.

In addition, Smith's commitment to being a great teammate and mentoring guys younger than him serves as a wonderful example that life is about having meaningful relationships without stepping on people on our way to the top. What a great way to live your life!

X. MENTORSHIP

We all need support and encouragement—
find a mentor, be a mentor

WE ALL WANT LOVE

A SUREFIRE SIGN OF PEOPLE with low self-esteem is their inability to admit when they are at fault. This is because they have often been made to feel inadequate, so admitting a mistake reinforces an upsetting feeling of inferiority. This is also the case with bullies, who try to make themselves look better by beating other people down. The greatest thing that can be offered to bullies and people who suffer from low esteem is love.

I had strong enough self-esteem as a high school football player to admit to Coach Hackett that it was my mistake of lining up under the guard that caused the fumble that squashed our final drive during the game he had attended when he was recruiting me. My self-confidence initially came from my parents, who always supported me, so much so that they took second jobs at night to pay for my high school tuition at Bishop Amat. They did this because they believed that if I got the opportunity to exhibit my talents with one of the best high school programs in Southern California, I might be able to get a scholarship to play football at a major university.

I would not have had the confidence to admit to Coach Hackett my mistake if I wasn't made to feel worthy by my parents and my coaches and teammates at Amat. And, after I arrived at USC to find myself ninth on a depth chart of nine quarterbacks, there is no way I would have risen to starter, All-American, and a career in the NFL without the support of Coach Hackett and the other USC coaches whose belief in me gave me the confidence to shine.

We all want someone who believes in us. We want someone who tells us we have what it takes to be great or tells us it's okay to do what we would like to do. This validation empowers us by offering encouragement, support, acceptance, and acknowledgment. It can be one person or any number of people—parents, family, spouse, friend, mentor, or teacher. All you need is just one of these individuals to give you the freedom to feel good enough about yourself, to believe enough in yourself, for you to take repeated action in whatever endeavor that moves you. Through these relationships, your confidence will build, and so will your self-belief.

Confidence, first and foremost, comes from taking the time to hone your craft. Through repetition, you can become an expert, no matter the job. And, when you couple these quality experiences with people along the way who support you, guide you, acknowledge you, and advocate for you, your path to success will be exponentially shorter.

So how do you find this special person who cares about you and your success?

I believe to attract this person(s) into your life, you must first have a sense of self-love. So, stop beating yourself up!

Be kind to yourself. If you develop a genuine self-love, then people will begin to appear in your path, mirroring these same feelings back to you. It is an energetic process.

Although I firmly believe that being a positive person will naturally attract people to help you, I also love the saying, "Don't ask, don't get." Not everybody is fortunate enough to be born into a family that supports them. Sometimes you might end up on a team, in a class, or at a job where the person in charge doesn't value your abilities. When coaching, teaching, or managing many people, it is easy to miss one or two in the group.

Ask for help! It is very challenging to make it in this world without the help of others. There are talents, life lessons, tools of the trade, and, most importantly, having someone in your corner that we all need. I strongly advise you to seek out mentors who can guide you along the way. If the person you ask doesn't respond, don't despair. There is a good chance that the current circumstances in their life prevent them from providing meaningful mentorship; however, many people are willing to help, so keep searching, and you will find the support you need.

The other way to attract a great mentor is to be a great mentor. People will notice your genuine willingness to help others and, when it is your turn to be helped, it will come. This is not a quid pro quo process where you volunteer to help someone because you want to use that as a chip that you can cash in to get your own help. Helping others is a gift, not a loan. Provide help with no strings attached, and the positive energy that you provide others will circle back.

Another good and practical benefit to volunteering is that it can dramatically expand your social and professional network. People who are decent enough to want to volunteer their time and money for charitable causes are exactly the individuals you want in your life. You will be friends with people who want to make their communities and the world a better place. What better circle of friends could you ask for than that?

As you endeavor to help others, it will lift your confidence because you will have the gratification of knowing that your talents are appreciated and that they are being used for the benefit of another. This joy in serving others for no other reason other than a genuine desire to help will consequently allow you to believe that you also deserve support.

Surrounding yourself on a daily basis with positive people is one of the best ways to create a life where you can both give and receive support. Be wise in selecting people who take the help you provide and will be there for you when you need it.

PICK YOUR TEAM

"NO MAN IS AN ISLAND." "Success breeds success." "A coach is only as good as his players."

There are tons of sayings and quotes which all point to a very simple concept—the best path to success is to surround yourself with good people. Think about it. You and your buddy are on the court getting ready to pick players for a playground hoops game. Are you going to give him all the first picks and take the players he doesn't want? Ah, no.

At work, a group of people often find every excuse in the book to make a trip to the watercooler and commiserate with others over how much they hate their job, how much the company sucks, and how awful the boss is. Start making regular trips to the watercooler, and there is a very good chance that pretty soon you, too, will start hating Monday mornings, and your path to any kind of success at that company will be stifled.

On many teams, there always seems to be a group of players who drift through practice. They prefer joking around and work just hard enough to get by but never push themselves to be better—to be the absolute best that they can be. Do you think joining this clique is going to help you to achieve your personal goals? Does this sound like a group that seems destined for championships?

In a previous chapter, we discussed the idea that you can't control what happens to you, but you can control how you choose to react to it. Likewise, you can make choices to surround yourself with people that will help you elevate yourself to a happier and more successful place.

One important aspect of life that cannot be ignored is that the people you spend lots of time with can play a massive role in the kind of life you end up having. Just like when you are on the playground picking a team, you should also consider your teammates for life that will help you be a better, more joyful, and productive person.

One key ingredient in attracting great teammates is to be a great teammate yourself. Will other people who are looking for high-quality friends want you for a teammate? Do they perceive you as someone who is only in it for themself—or someone who will be there for them when they need you and cheer for them when they have their own victories?

"I'd rather lose than watch the way some kids play. I'd rather lose....They're always thinking about themselves. Me, me, me, I didn't score, so why should I be happy? I'm not getting enough minutes; why should I be happy? That's the world we live in today, unfortunately."[112]

Those words were spoken by University of Connecticut women's basketball coach Geno Auriemma at a post-game press conference during the 2017 NCAA championship tournament. Coach Geno is a legend in the world of hoops. He has won eleven NCAA national championships, the most in women's college basketball history. He has coached two Olympic gold-winning basketball teams and has been awarded the national Naismith College Coach of the Year award an amazing eight times.[113]

When Coach Geno speaks, people listen. It's no surprise that his words at a pair of post-game press conferences during that tournament became viral YouTube sensations. The subject he ranted about was the high degree of importance that he and his staff place on having a team filled with good teammates.

Here are some excerpts from one of Coach Geno's press conferences:

"Recruiting enthusiastic kids is harder than it's ever been.... Recruiting kids that are really upbeat, loving life, love the game, and have this tremendous appreciation for when their teammates do something well, that's hard (to find)...so on our team, we, me, my coaching staff, we put a huge premium on body language.... When I watch game film, I'm checking what's going on on the bench. If somebody's asleep over there, if somebody doesn't care, if somebody's not engaged in the game, they will never get in the game, ever! And they know that. They know I'm not kidding."[114]

Coach Geno is a man that has a cabinet jammed full of trophies and medals from the most prestigious tournaments that women's basketball has to offer, and yet he readily acknowledges that he would rather lose than put players on the court who have a bad attitude. Do you think maybe his stubborn principles might have something to do with his success?

Does Coach Geno seem like the kind of guy that would recruit the complainers at the watercooler or the drifters at practice? If a guy who is a proven champion wouldn't recruit these kids to his team, why would you recruit them to yours? And more importantly, why would you let yourself become someone that other people recruiting their life teammates wouldn't want for those same reasons?

One word of caution when you are thinking about the life team you are picking—you should definitely consider finding friends who share academic or career interests so you can develop a great professional network to help you achieve your goals. However, the team you pick should never exclusively be just about academic standing or career aspirations.

A quality team is a group of people who will love you, even when the chips are down. Your team should include people who provide you spiritual strength and guidance, who make you laugh, who share a passion for your hobbies and interests, who are people you can trust. Your team should have a well-balanced group of friends with the common denominator being that they are all high-quality people.

Your goal every day should be to be the best person you can be and to surround yourself with other people who want to live life the right way. Do this, and miracles can happen.

The values that Coach Geno looks for in picking his teams have been tried and true for generations. From old school guys like Coach Lombardi with the Packers and Coach Wooden at UCLA to modern greats such as Coach K at Duke and Coach

Belichick with the Patriots, they all realize that great people lead to great success.

I cannot emphasize enough how important it is to follow their lead and surround yourself with an amazing group of friends that can help you be better. However, remember, it goes both ways, and being a great friend means doing the same for them. Be a great teammate!

BE A GREAT
TEAMMATE

LEADING MY TEAM TO VICTORY by making key throws in big moments of games has blessed me with some of my greatest thrills in football. At USC, I completed touchdown passes against powerhouses LSU, Notre Dame, and Alabama, crosstown rival UCLA, as well as Michigan and Ohio State in Rose Bowls. However, these joys were no comparison to watching my oldest son, Michael, throw his first touchdown pass as a Trojan quarterback twenty-five years later.

Michael was a gifted athlete with exceptional hand-eye coordination, which allowed him to excel in every sport he played as a child and throughout his high school career. Randomly, he started playing volleyball for the first time as a ninth-grader and ultimately became a starter as a senior at one of the most prominent programs in Southern California, Newport Harbor High School. Today, he's close to a scratch golfer after only playing seriously for the last seven years. To the competitive McDonald family, it's annoying, to say the least, because he makes it look so easy.

Michael's real love was football (I wonder where that came from). After only starting one year at quarterback his senior year, he really wanted to attend USC to continue playing football. Although he didn't receive a scholarship offer, he decided to attend as a preferred walk-on. It's no surprise because Troy was in his blood—his grandparents, Roger and Marilyn, both attended USC, as did his mom and I.

Michael grew up going to games as a boy and fell in love with everything about the place. It was impossible for him to resist the pull even though he was not a recruited athlete. His dream was the dream of most college walk-ons, show the coaches your stuff and earn the scholarship that was not offered while still playing in high school. My son had a lot of confidence in his ability to perform, and he believed he would be able to earn his way onto the starting roster of a program full of star players from across the country.

Reality soon set in.

It was not as easy as he thought it was going to be. To become the starting quarterback as a preferred walk-on at a legendary program like USC is extremely rare because you are competing against highly sought-after four- and five-star recruits. It would take time, patience, and a lot of luck. So, after two years toiling on the scout squad (the players who replicate the opposing team in practice) and fighting for reps, Michael made the difficult decision to leave the program to concentrate more on school and the career he would be pursuing after graduation. The battle to garner the attention of the coaches and get playing time, or even to feel like he was a contributor to the team, became too great of a hill to climb.

Soon after Michael left the football program, I was approached on campus by the USC quarterbacks' coach, Steve Sarkisian. He indicated to me that the team really needed Michael to come back for the 2005 spring practice. For a variety of reasons, there was a significant scarcity of players available at quarterback.

Spring practice plays a crucial role in preparing players and the team for the upcoming season and doing it with a shortage of quarterbacks posed a big problem. Michael's return would make the sessions much more productive. Although his participation would help the team, Michael would still be on the outside looking in when the next season began—a walk-on getting very few reps during practice and probably no playing time during games. Michael was aware of this, but the team was in a bind, so he agreed to put his next chapter on hold for a minute and return for the spring sessions to help his teammates get better.

The issue in sports and society today is that people generally ask themselves, "What's in it for me?" Whether it's a job assignment or a favor for a friend, the tendency is to weigh the "ask" against what we would receive in return. In other words, why would I answer the bell if there wasn't a pot of gold for me at the end of the rainbow?

Know this—giving freely of oneself without expecting something in return is a very spiritual quality. It is a characteristic that is challenging to find in our world where me, me, and more me is the focus. How refreshing is it when you find a friend that you know you can count on without having to keep score of favors asked and given? Interestingly, I really believe that when operating in a more freely giving manner, the returns we receive in life tend to exceed our expectations, and they often manifest in surprising ways.

In returning to the USC football team, Michael placed his own personal desires on hold, knowing that he would be returning to more of the same unfulfilled environment he had recently left: extensive weight training, conditioning, film-room work, and unglamorous practice time running the scout team, which would probably go unnoticed. In other words, the chance of him accomplishing his goal of playing a significant role for the Trojans was still the same—zero percent! Honestly, he was just an extra arm that was needed to allow the team to have more efficient practices.

Michael opted to be a great teammate and help his guys out with no expectation of anything in return other than maybe a thank you for supporting them. After spring ball was over, Michael felt like his duties to the team were completed. He again decided to quit football, and then something incredible happened.

It was early June, and Michael was on his bike riding to the beach when his cell phone rang. It was the Trojans head coach, Pete Carroll. Pete began selling Michael on the program and imploring him to return. Oh, by the way, at the end of the discussion, Pete sweetened the deal by offering Michael something that every walk-on dreams of, but only a few achieve—a full-ride scholarship. Michael accepted, accomplishing one of his biggest goals when deciding to attend USC.

We all want love!

Being a scholarship athlete instead of a walk-on was validation that Michael was really wanted on the team. He now felt part of the family instead of feeling like he was on the outside looking in. Another benefit was his dad just got a big pay increase because now the USC athletic department was paying his tuition and expenses. The McDonald's were all incredibly happy!

It wasn't just the joy of saving a lot on tuition. As most parents will understand, seeing my kid get a chance to step onto the field and live out one of his dreams was far better for me than anything I did when playing football. The second game of 2005 was at home against Arkansas. The Trojans dominated the Razorbacks, leading 63–17 when Michael trotted onto the field with a couple of minutes left to play. I was broadcasting the game alongside my partner, Pete Arbogast, and almost fell out of the booth knowing how far he had come in just a few short months.

USC had the ball on the Arkansas twenty-seven-yard line, and Michael was handing the ball off to run out the clock, but he was on the field for the first time under center, so it was a thrill! The Trojans got the ball to the five-yard line, third down and three yards to go when, much to the surprise of everyone in the coliseum, Michael suddenly dropped back to pass. This is not something you typically do in a blowout game, so I think it was a way for the offensive coaches to say "thank you" to Michael for the favor he provided the prior spring.

As Michael looked for an open receiver, the pocket was starting to close, so he threw the ball to the only place his tight end could catch it, low and away. Jimmy Miller stretched out and made a great catch for the touchdown! There was euphoria on the field (and in the broadcast booth!) when the official put both hands in the air indicating a touchdown. Michael had completed his first pass for a touchdown at the end of a game where the outcome had long been decided, but it didn't matter. This moment signified what can happen when you give of yourself to others without expecting anything in return. It was a just reward to Michael for being a selfless teammate.

For three seasons, Michael was the holder for field goals and extra points and completed a crucial touchdown pass on a fake field goal to beat Washington in 2006. At that juncture, his first two passes were both touchdowns, which is undoubtedly an NCAA record! He also saw the field as a quarterback in many other games, including UCLA and the Rose Bowl. He got a chance to be a scholarship player on USC teams that played in three Rose Bowls, winning two, a pretty amazing thing that very few people who have played football ever got to experience.

Giving of oneself for the benefit of others, with no strings attached, is a powerful way to live. When your purpose is outside your own ego, good things will circle back to you. This is a spiritual way to operate in life. So, be a great teammate, do something unsolicited for your team, family, friends, or community, and you will surely be rewarded unexpectedly with something far greater than what you gave, just like my son Michael learned during his USC football career. He's got the Rose Bowl rings to prove it!

OUR GREATEST GIFT

THROUGHOUT THE HISTORY of college football, there is no bigger holiday on the calendar than New Year's Day. This is the time when powerhouses like USC, Alabama, Clemson, and Oklahoma compete in legendary bowl games, such as the Rose Bowl, Sugar Bowl, Orange Bowl, and Fiesta Bowl.

In the 2003 Fiesta Bowl, the Ohio State Buckeyes defeated the Miami Hurricane 31–24 to win the game and the national championship. One of the stars on the field that day for the Buckeyes was running back Maurice Clarett, who ran for two touchdowns, including the game-winner in the second overtime of the instant classic.[115]

Three years later, Ohio State was back in the Fiesta Bowl and, at the exact time the Buckeyes were on the field defeating Notre Dame 34–20, Clarett was in a police station, turning himself in after he had been accused of armed robbery. Eight months later, in September of 2006, Clarett was sentenced to prison.[116]

At the sentencing hearing, a statement from one of the robbery victims was read in court. "Mr. Clarett, we hope you will use this opportunity to help someone along the way."[117]

Helping others is exactly what Maurice Clarett has done.

Prior to arriving at Ohio State, Clarett grew up in Youngstown, Ohio. In his book, *One and Done*, Clarett describes his hometown. There was a lot of crime and killings. The gangs in Youngstown at the time were really heavy. He recalled that the first time he personally saw someone murdered, he was only ten years old.[118]

Clarett soon took to a life on the streets; drinking, getting high, stealing cars, robbing stores, and selling drugs. He was already placed in juvenile detention three times before even finishing middle school and was only saved from a permanent life in jail because he could play football. By the time Clarett's senior season of high school football rolled around, he was being recruited by every major college football program in the nation before settling on Ohio State.

A few months after leading Ohio State to the national championship, trouble reappeared in Clarett's life. The NCAA investigated him for an incident where more than $10,000 worth of clothing, cash, CDs, and stereo equipment was stolen from a car that Clarett had borrowed from a dealership in Ohio. He was later charged for lying to the police on the theft report and was suspended from Ohio State for the 2003 season.[119]

Taken away from football, Clarett's life spiraled out of control. While appearing on NBC's *Today* show to promote *One and Done*, Clarett described what happened. "I got a ton of violations and they eventually suspended me. The next thing you know I was substituting by drinking, drugging."[120]

Clarett went on to explain the dark place he had entered when he was kicked off the team. "When you're going through your despair, I think that you have these self-defeating thoughts that, you know, 'This will be the rest of my life.'" He added, "You're looking at life like it's just this endless despair or just this confusing place."[121]

Clarett's downward spiral of drugs, drinking, and crime hit rock-bottom when he was arrested and placed in jail. Although prison is not a path that should be recommended to anyone, the pause in his life gave Clarett the opportunity to evaluate who he was and where he wanted to go. He became a student of life. He told the interviewer on *Today*, "When I was in prison I went through a bunch of therapeutic services and I think that's what really changed my life, just becoming self-reflective and gaining skills to govern myself."[122]

Nearly four years after being locked up, Clarett walked out a free man. He said, "When I got out of prison, I was on a mission, a vow to help people."[123]

Clarett found that the best way he could help people was to tell his story. His talks are designed to steer the audience away from repeating the mistakes he made or uplifting the ones who are hurting to believe that they can rise out of their despair. These stories are especially relatable for young athletes from disen-franchised neighborhoods and for men serving time in prison.

It turns out the man can talk. Clarett has become a highly sought-after guest with more than four hundred speaking appearances at universities and organizations.

Clarett took the money he earned from those talks to invest back into his hometown. Even though he had a tough upbringing, Clarett has always had a deep love for Youngstown. His dedication to his hometown and desire to help people suffering from the same challenges he faced inspired him to start The Red Zone, a mental health counseling and substance abuse agency.[124] In his book, Clarett summed up his desire to help people by saying that he had found his purpose in life. He was put on this earth to aid people in their healing process and get better.[125]

The trials and tribulations that Clarett went through allowed him to understand the pain that many other people are experiencing and give them firsthand advice on how to find the light at the end of the tunnel. His greatest effectiveness comes from the very fact that he felt the same pain that they are now suffering.

It has been said that some shaman healers physically break every bone in their own body, so they can truly understand what it feels like to treat someone with a particular ailment. Through this dramatic self-flagellation, the shamans will be better able to relate to the physical, mental, and emotional distress encountered by another because they have had the exact same experience. There is a direct connection between the healer and the patient.

When we come from a similar background and have the same experiences as another, we are bonded. We search for this bond when meeting someone for the very first time. While communicating with this new acquaintance, we always look for some commonality to create a connection to decide if there is enough stickiness to hang around.

Sometimes that commonality can be a joyful one, such as recalling the championship season of a shared favorite team. Other times it can be painful, such as when we console a friend who has lost a loved one by letting them know we understand the hurt they feel because we also have lost loved ones. In those times of sadness, our own pain is a gift that can be shared to comfort and ease the pain of others.

Pain that is experienced in this lifetime is not exclusive. Many, many others have generally lived through similar situations. Also, this painful feeling comes with powerful emotions. These emotions remain with us as fuel to propel us in the positive or in the negative. In other words, if we cannot positively channel these emotions emanating from the pain we endured, they will remain with us to relive the experience again and again. However, if we can turn lemons into lemonade by constructively taking these lessons learned from our own painful experiences to assist humanity in dealing with similar pains, then we will transcend it.

Think back on your most painful experiences in life. Wouldn't it be great to utilize your knowledge and wisdom garnered from such pain to repurpose it to help others? My guess is there would be nothing more gratifying than to help or even save another human being. And, in the process, you would be saving yourself.

Through the work that Maurice Clarett is doing to help others at his mental health and substance recovery agency, it could easily be said that the person he is most helping is himself. What a wonderful gift he has been given!

XI. A FULFILLED LIFE

Live life with purpose—love, be compassionate, and serve others

PLAYING WITH
PURPOSE

THE 2019 WNBA CHAMPIONSHIP came down to the very last quarter of the season. The Washington Mystics and Connecticut Sun were tied two games each going into the final game of the best-of-five championship series. The Sun led by two points entering the fourth quarter.[126]

It was time for Elena Delle Donne to shine.

Earlier in the playoffs, Delle Donne had been named the league MVP for the second time in her seven-year WNBA career. However, in game two of the series, Delle Donne suffered painful back spasms, which caused her to miss most of the game. She returned in game three and gritted her way through a thirteen-point performance, followed by eleven points in game four. This was far below her career average of 20.3 points per game, but understandable when it was later revealed that she was playing with three herniated discs.[127]

Delle Donne entered the decisive fifth game of the series with not only the pain of a back injury but the memory of having been in a final series twice before, only to lose both times. Would Delle Donne be able to deliver a performance that would finally allow her and her teammates to hoist the trophy at the end of a season? The answer was a resounding yes.

Delle Donne had a massive game five with nine rebounds and twenty-one points, including four key points during an 8–0 Mystics run with three minutes left in the game, which secured the victory and the championship. The accolades came pouring in after Delle Donne's gutsy performance to secure the championship, with some social commentators calling her the best women's basketball player in the world. Ironically, she almost stopped playing the sport after a prolific high school career.[128]

Delle Donne was a much-heralded high school basketball star while attending Ursuline Academy in Delaware with scholarship offers from numerous major college basketball programs such as Duke, Tennessee, and Notre Dame. She ultimately chose NCAA powerhouse Connecticut, coached by Geno Auriemma, who has won eleven NCAA D-1 college basketball championships, more than any coach in history.[129]

In the summer of 2008, only two days after first arriving on the Connecticut campus, Delle Donne quit basketball.

Delle Donne drove through the night to arrive home around midnight and tell her parents that she was leaving Connecticut. She had come to deeply resent basketball because it was taking her away from her family, and, as she explained in various subsequent interviews on the subject, Delle Donne loved her family more than she loved basketball.[130]

Delle Donne grew up very close to her family, especially to her older sister, Lizzie. Born with autism and cerebral palsy, as well as being deaf and blind, Lizzie's only way of communicating with people is through touch. The bond that Delle Donne has with her sister is incredibly strong and, because she couldn't call or Skype to communicate with Lizzie, the move to Connecticut to play basketball was that much harder.

Adding to Delle Donne's burden was that basketball had become an expectation and not a joy. She was such a major star player in high school, with so many scholarship offers. It was everyone's assumption that she would continue playing basketball without anyone ever stopping to think if that was something she really wanted to do.[131]

Delle Donne decided to stay closer to home by attending Delaware University and take a break from basketball. However, she did walk-on to the volleyball team, where she played as a freshman before the pull to play basketball began to reemerge. Delle Donne started going into the gym to take shots, and she came to realize how much she enjoyed playing. It felt good to shoot a basketball.[132]

Although Delle Donne began to understand that she loved playing, a gnawing guilt still stayed with her. She felt it was completely unfair that she could go out and play while her sister Lizzie, who she loved so much, was confined by her disabilities. In an interview with Indiana newspaper, *The Elkhart Truth*, Delle Donne explained. "I went through a time where it was very tough for me to be an athlete and to be able do so many things, things that Lizzie couldn't."[133]

In the same interview, Delle Donne recalled a conversation she had that completely changed her perspective. She said, "It really wasn't until I met a lady with cerebral palsy at Lizzie's school who told me, 'Do everything you can with your abilities, just like we do.'"[134]

This simple revelation took away Delle Donne's guilt, and it gave her a purpose. She was no longer just playing for herself; she was now playing for Lizzie, and everyone like her, who were not able to go out on the court themselves. Just like they were doing the very best with what they had, Delle Donne would do all that she could do to be her own personal best self.

David Hawkins writes in *Power vs. Force* that true power arises from meaning. It has to do with motive and principle. Power appeals to what uplifts. It dignifies and makes us feel positive about ourselves because of the greater good that it is serving. Our greatest power comes from within when we do what we love, what we are good at, and when we use our gifts for a greater purpose.[135]

Delle Donne unleashed her power when she rediscovered her joy for playing basketball and began using her gifts to play for her sister, Lizzie, and everyone else stricken with autism and cerebral palsy.

In his book, Hawkins continues by describing the meaning of force. Force must always be justified. Force is being manipulative and imposing your will on others in a negative way. It is also willing something to happen that isn't the natural best fit. Think of it as trying to pound a square peg into a round hole. Oftentimes, an indication of forcing something to happen is doing things in life that don't bring you joy, not being in alignment with who you are, or lacking some form of higher-self purpose.[136]

The question you must first answer, though, is why do you want what you want? What is the underlying reason pushing you to take action? If it is powerful enough, it will take an army to hold you back. However, if you're simply using will-power to muscle through another job, your success rate will probably be limited, and your happiness level will most likely be subpar. It is not a sustainable way to live.

Those things that have the greatest meaning for us do not originate from the material world that says, "What's in it for me?" Instead, real empowerment and meaning come from looking outside of self, like Delle Donne learned when she met the lady with cerebral palsy at her sister's school.

If the motivation within is strong enough, you can change! You can create new habits and a new life by entering the arena for the first time or re-entering it again and again. Motivation is the energy that drives us all to execute, to get things done. It doesn't matter; if the objective is to win a game, get a job, finish a project, or get sober, you must be inspired to bring something significant to fruition.

When our purpose for undertaking an endeavor is centered on family, community, a nation, or just the pure enjoyment of performing a skill you were gifted with, then you are operating from a source of true power.[137]

It is all within you and accessible by you. But, you must commit to diving inward to understand what provides the most meaning in your life and use that as your motivation every day when you decide to go for it, again!

The ultimate question we must all answer in our lifetime is why are we here? Is it to gather a cabinet full of trophies and a house full of material things? Or is it to be a person that is a great daughter, brother, mother, husband, or person who commits to making their community a better place?

Here is the secret that very few people will tell you—when a big part of your motivation is to help others, the light within you will shine much more brightly, and the person you will most help is yourself. There is nothing that can build your self-belief more than knowing you are playing with purpose. Miracles can happen. You can reach your dreams. And when you make your life a team game, instead of an individual game, the greatest champion will be you.

Go win that championship! You deserve it!

CHAMPIONSHIP WON, NOW WHAT?

IMAGINE PURSUING A GOAL for most of your life, and then you finally achieve it. What's next?

The Liverpool Football Club is one of the most famous and popular sports teams in the world. Whenever the team travels to any point on the globe, there are typically tens of thousands of red-clad fans who serenade the players with the club's anthem, "You'll Never Walk Alone."

Although they are one of the most successful soccer clubs on the planet, Liverpool was in a massive drought in English football. They had not won an English soccer league championship for thirty years until 2020 when they were finally able to lift the English Premier League trophy.[138]

One of Liverpool's biggest stars in their championship season was Sadio Mané. The star forward hails from Senegal, one of the poorest nations in the world. The annual median household income in Senegal is only $3,897, approximately the amount that an average American household earns in in a month.[139] As a star player in one of the top soccer clubs in the world, Mané makes in one week the same as the average Senegalese household makes in thirty-five years![140]

It was not an easy path to become a global soccer superstar for Mané. In an interview with Joe Dada of the Ghanaian media outlet *Nsemwoha,* Mané explained, "I was hungry, and I had to work in the field; I survived hard times, played football barefooted, I did not have an education and many other things."[141]

It would be easy for someone like Mané, who came from such an impoverished background, to splurge when the championships have been won, and the riches have finally arrived. What do you think winning a championship would do for your life? Would you finally get that sports car, private jet, or diamond-studded watch? The contemporary version of success often features these images to portray the ultimate winner.

Mané, who had nothing and now has everything, decided to avoid the trap of a bling-bling lifestyle and instead do something more meaningful with his new fortune. In the same article, he stated, "Why would I want ten Ferraris, twenty diamond watches, or two planes? What will these objects do for me and for the world?"[142] Mané added, "I built schools, a stadium, we provide clothes, shoes, food for people who are in extreme poverty. In addition, I give 70 euros per month to all people in a very poor region of Senegal which contributes to their family economy. I do not need to display luxury cars, luxury homes, trips and even planes. I prefer that my people receive a little of what life has given me."[143]

The ultimate question for every human being is—why am I here? Is it to earn a lot of money and to become rich? The short answer is no. Is it to be famous where people across the planet recognize us because we were on the big screen or television? The answer, once again, is no. Is it to be able to control the lives of others by virtue of a position we hold? The answer, in my opinion, is no!

For many people, money, fame, and power are the ultimate goals in life. What could be better than having just one of these to lead a completely fulfilled life? I'm not saying money, fame, and power are not worthwhile objectives. However, they should not be the end game. They should simply be byproducts of doing what you love.

What matters is how you feel about the byproducts that you earn from all of your work doing what you love. Do you become so fascinated with money that you care more about it than your own children? Do you love being famous more than having a simple conversation with a lifelong friend? And, do you love ordering people around but won't take the trash out at home?

If so, you have lost perspective.

Sometimes, in the hot pursuit of achievement, we lose ourselves and our perception of what's important. Sooner or later, if everyone is telling us how great we are, we start to believe it. We start to believe we are better than the next person. This attitude will fuel our ego for more, but it could also lead to emptiness, loneliness, and unhappiness. It's easy to get so caught up in the idea of fame and fortune that we lose sight of the most important things in life, especially when those things arrive.

To whom much is given, much is expected is a principle found in the bible that aptly describes why we are here. The way Mané lives his life embodies this quote. He refused to allow himself to become enraptured with material things or his status as a global soccer star, but instead, he has focused his energy on sharing his success with his people. Believe me, this use of his wealth brings infinitely more joy than a luxury car or flashy jewelry.

What feeds the soul is using your platform of success, whatever that may mean to you, to elevate your family, neighborhood, community, and society at large. We are here to use our personal gifts and resources to lift others. This is what I believe, and if this belief was commonplace, the world would be a better place. It is on all of us to do our part by acknowledging others, having compassion for them, and taking action by gifting our own precious resources—time and money.

At the highest level, we are all on this planet with one mission—to evolve! That's a relative statement because we all entered this life at our own unique level, and we do not arrive as a finished product. It doesn't matter what level at which we arrive. Here's what truly matters: Are we growing, improving, and moving up the evolutionary barometer towards humility, compassion, and love?

What level are you at on your path? A championship is a material metric, but where are you on the most important things that measure a person in life?

BALANCE

PLAYING CATCH is the quintessential American pastime. Tossing the ball back and forth in the backyard with mom, dad, or a sibling is often the first experience many kids have in sports. Some do it with a ball and glove, others with a football, but for those who are fortunate enough to have had those moments, they are often the most prized memories we have. It is why so many men weep when they see the scene where Kevin Costner gets to play catch again with the ghost of his dad in the movie *Field of Dreams*.

My *Field of Dreams* moment, which brought me to tears, happened with my son Michael on Senior Day, his last home game in the coliseum as a USC quarterback.

It all started four years before, in 2003, during the start of Michael's freshman season. I was the analyst for radio broadcasts of USC football games, and I was on the field during pre-game when I noticed head coach, Pete Carroll, playing catch with his son, the USC tight ends coach, Brennan Carroll, (as they did before every game). My initial thought was, "How cool is that!" My next one was, "Why can't I do this with my son?" And so I suggested to Michael that we play catch during pre-game warm-ups. Thankfully, he agreed.

We threw it around during every home game, and when Michael started traveling during the '04 season, we played catch everywhere—from South Bend to Pro Player Stadium during the national championship game against Oklahoma to the many Rose Bowls played by the Trojans during his college career. Tossing the ball around those amazing stadiums with my son was like a backyard game of catch on steroids. They are some of my most cherished memories.

When a person is nearing their final days, what do you think they'd do if they could go back in time? Spend another day at the office or have one more game of catch with their kid? I think you would probably agree that a vast majority would choose to play catch. So, if doing something as simple as tossing a ball with your kid is so meaningful to so many people, why do so many forgo doing that for extra time at work?

Is it worth winning the Super Bowl or any other major accolade if you don't have any friends or family with whom to share the victory? Is it worth becoming CEO of a Fortune 500 company if you work so many hours that you end up in the hospital with a life-threatening illness? Of course not. However, because we all get caught up in the rat race of our society, we forget to have a life.

Where we place our focus and attention, so goes our energy. The challenge with western society is that we compensate those who are specialists, those who have unique, exceptional skills, those who set themselves apart from the pack—and we view them as a success. They are experts, not generalists.

For many to achieve such designation in one area of their life, they must sacrifice all else to attain their dream, but usually at a significant cost. The cost may be their kids, spouse, friends, peace of mind, or possibly their life. In our culture, our focus and energy are often placed on our work life to accumulate prizes and show everyone how truly special we are. There is nothing wrong with money! But, if you are focusing your life exclusively on acquiring things, you will surely destroy yourself.

There is a time and a place for everything in life. When I was in training camp playing football, it was a 24/7 all-in month-long experience. There wasn't any time for family, friends, or hobbies. There was only football during that part of the year. The key here is that camp was for a finite number of weeks.

There are times when focus and energy must completely be dedicated to only one endeavor because it requires such an inordinate amount of attention. It might be starting a new business, writing a book, or caring for a loved one who is ill. Whatever the reason for this intense commitment, we must always remember that moderation is the key. We can't continue to pour our energy exclusively into only one aspect of life, or we risk burnout or any number of other illnesses. At some point in time, we must come up for air to fully experience all aspects of life.

Having balance is not only a good thing, it is essential. However, this doesn't mean you can't have it all. I am here to tell you that you can! You can have great relationships with family and friends that you value. You can have excellent personal health by getting the optimal amount of sleep, eating the appropriate quality foods, working out enough to stay fit, and recreating with those activities that bring you joy. You can have superior emotional and spiritual health by maintaining a positive mindset, meditating, journaling, taking a walk, going to church, or creating memorable events in your life. You can make an impact in this world and feel better about yourself because you are giving back to your community through your favorite charity or non-profit. Oh, and yes, you can also have a rewarding career.

It does take a concentrated commitment, but you can have balance in your life.

When I was younger, I worked far too many hours, and my family life suffered. I was on a mission to make it. In the process, I almost lost my wife, Allyson, and missed out on many opportunities to see my children perform or just be with them. This lifestyle drove me to the dark place that required me to make a mid-life adjustment.

When I started to understand what I was missing, I opened my eyes and became conscious. I took a USC game off from broadcasting because it was dangerously close to my son Matthew's due date, and I did not want to miss his birth. I also missed the broadcast of a Notre Dame game to walk my daughter, Stephanie, down the aisle at her debutante ball. And, I finally retired from broadcasting USC football games to watch Andrew's senior season as starting quarterback for New Mexico State.

There are lots of people who might have seen those decisions as major sacrifices. Anybody who has been around Trojans football for even a short while knows how massive the Notre Dame game is. There are legions of former athletes who would give anything to have the opportunity to call games for a powerhouse program like USC. When I look back on those decisions, I don't see them as sacrifices; I see them as some of the best choices I ever made. I only wish I had figured it out sooner.

Do not make the same mistakes I made! You don't have to wait until later in life to start prioritizing who and what is important to you. A well-balanced life is crucial to one's overall health and well-being. So, step out of the race for a day or two, ponder what is most important to you, and begin to create the balanced life you have always dreamed of.

Fortunately, Michael learned to find balance as a much younger dad than me. He is a great example of what leading a balanced life is all about. He works, yes, but that does not consume him. He always finds time for his amazing wife, Lauren, and for playing with and teaching his three boys how to live and have fun. Michael also does a great job of having his "me" time working out or smacking the ball around the golf course or listening to one of his favorite health and wellness podcasts while driving to a meeting.

And so, back to Senior Day 2007 for Michael's last home game in the coliseum. It happened to be against UCLA, just like my last home game in 1979. It was also the last time we were able to toss the ball at the coliseum. As I made my last throw for a touchdown to Michael, I thought back to those touchdowns I threw to Kevin Williams, Calvin Sweeney, Danny Garcia, Vic Rakhshani, etc., during my playing days on this same turf nearly thirty years before.

No pass I ever threw in college or the NFL was as emotional as this one.

I walked over to give my son one last hug and wish him luck before he entered the locker room in final preparation for the game. I told him how much it had meant to me that he allowed me to play catch with him during the four years of his college career. His simple response brought tears to my eyes. "It meant a lot to me too, Dad."

You don't have to play catch on the floor of the coliseum to have your *Field of Dreams* moment—you have to choose to make the time to have it. You will love it!

LOVE AND SERVE

SPORTS FANS AND JOURNALISTS love to debate who the all-time best player of a sport might be. In basketball, the most often mentioned candidates are Michael Jordan, Kareem Abdul-Jabbar, Magic Johnson, Larry Bird, and Kobe Bryant. I would argue it is LeBron James. In tennis, my pick would be Roger Federer, and in football, Warrick Dunn.

My Lebron and Roger picks might generate some heated debate, but at least people would see them as being in the conversation. However, they would all think I lost my mind in mentioning Warrick Dunn. Many people might even ask, "Who the hell is Warrick Dunn?" Let me tell you.

Dunn played college football at Florida State and was chosen by the Baltimore Ravens with the twelfth overall pick in the first round of the 1997 NFL Draft. Dunn had a great football career. In college, he was a second-team All-American and national champion with the Seminoles, and in the NFL, he was the Offensive Rookie of the Year in 1997 and was a three-time Pro Bowl selection.[144]

Dunn's on-the-field accomplishments are definitely impressive, but is he in the GOAT category for yards gained, touchdowns scored, championships won? Of course not.

Dunn's true greatness came off the field. Just days after Dunn turned eighteen, his mother, an off-duty police officer, was murdered while escorting a businesswoman to make a night deposit. Dunn was forced to become the man of the house and raise his siblings while he attended college and played football at Florida State.[145]

Inspired by how hard his single mom worked to put a roof over the family's head, Dunn leveraged the good fortune he received from playing professional football into helping others in the same position that his mother was in when she was still alive. In 1997, Dunn launched Home for the Holidays, a charity that surprises hard-working single parents with a fully furnished house (and pantry) and even the down payment to purchase the house.[146]

To date, Dunn's charity has placed 180 families into new homes.[147] Dunn explained his feelings about his charity to Monique Welch of the *Tampa Bay Times*. "I've used this program as therapy. Every time I hand over those keys there's a little piece of my mom and the things she wanted."[148]

Ask any of the 180 families that are in a home because of Dunn's dedication to serving who they think is football's GOAT, and they will tell you, Warrick Dunn! And so will I.

Likewise, ask the same GOAT question for basketball to the thousands of students in Akron, Ohio, who are receiving fully covered college scholarships due to LeBron James' partnerships with Akron University and Kent State. It's pretty easy to guess that the King is their king.

My personal all-time favorite tennis player (and, for that matter, any sport) is easily Roger Federer. I admire how he conducts himself as an athlete and as a family man. My preferences aside, what makes him the GOAT in tennis? Just like LeBron, it is his dedication to education. To date, Roger's foundation has spent over $52 million to provide over 1.5 million students in Switzerland and various African nations with access to better education.[149]

These are the debates we should be having when discussing the various candidates for GOAT. Let's not just look at their accomplishments between the lines but consider how they are able to translate their game-time wins into real-world victories by serving others. The sports page should honestly place philanthropic rankings right next to the AP Top 25 in college football or the standings for all the professional sports leagues.

And lest you think that you are off the hook to do charity work until you are a rich and famous professional athlete, think again. You can start giving back at an early age by doing community clean-ups, tutoring younger students, or visiting the elderly at nursing homes. You can also do things at home that no one outside your family notices but make all the difference in the world.

These little acts of kindness, performed in private when no one is watching, speak volumes as to how evolved you are. There is no PR campaign or press release to announce it publicly. It's just you and your intention to make a difference in someone else's life that is the motivation.

The ultimate and highest representation of living an elevated life is loving and serving. It's giving of yourself to better the lives of others. There are many examples of loving and serving, but I believe the most natural and instinctual form of this higher-self model is that of motherhood.

Mothers are love!

Mothers carry a child in their womb for forty weeks until they are delivered. By the way, no man would ever want to endure any type of childbirth pain. I know this because I have personally seen four of my own children delivered before my very eyes, and I would not want any part of it!

As painful as delivery might be, a mother's work is only getting started in the maternity ward. They are typically the captain of the ship when it comes to raising the children in their household. A mother teaches children all they know and encourages them to grow up to be the best person possible. They often give up many of their own interests and make numerous sacrifices for their children. From the very first days, when crying babies are up at all hours, needing to be fed and cleaned, to the teenage years, when late-night calls require waking up to provide a safe ride home, there are no limits on what a mother will do for her son or daughter.

I know this to be true because I am married to one of the greatest mothers of all time, Allyson.

While I was attempting to take over the business world, Allyson was the one who spent the most time raising and managing our children's lives, and she was incredible at it. She helped with schoolwork and was always available to listen to whatever they wanted to talk about. There were countless carpools, driving the kids to school, various practices and games for the boys, and dance recitals for Stephanie. There were many road trips to Catalina Island for summer fun and Snow Summit to ski, where she packed for everyone, shopped for food, and did the cooking. She was a workhorse, and it was always perfect.

Over the years, Allyson has many times cared for her dad after he sustained injuries or had one of his many surgeries. And recently, Andrew and Matthew both stayed with us after separate surgeries to have their mom nurse them back to health. Preparing their food, medications, and administering treatments for them was just a sampling of what she provided. The real secret sauce was simply caring for and loving them. There is nothing like a mom taking care of you when you don't feel well, even after you've reached adulthood.

The best example of Allyson loving and serving others is when she graciously welcomed my mom, Annie, to come live with us after she fractured her wrist in a car accident.

The accident happened just before my mom's eighty-ninth birthday, and it soon became evident that she shouldn't be driving. It was no longer practical for my mom to continue living in her house without being able to drive. She wouldn't be able to drive to the pharmacist, her doctor's appointments, the grocery store, and so on. She was going to leave the house she had lived in for fifty-two years, the house I was raised in, and my mom made it very clear she would never move into any sort of senior assisted living arrangement. We tried, but she was a stubborn Russian who would not budge. There was only one option left—move in with us.

My mother had no filter. She was blunt and said exactly what was on her mind when speaking about herself or others, including family. Also, from the first time she met Allyson when we were dating, and for years later, she wasn't really warm and fuzzy around her. It may have been a mother-son thing, but it occasionally created friction that annoyed my wife.

With this as the back story to their relationship, it was a big ask to have my mom move in, especially because we knew that it would be Allyson doing the lion's share of caring for her, bathing her, and tending to her needs. Not to mention, at the time, we were temporarily living in a smaller two-bedroom rental home where there wasn't much space to escape for "Allyson Time." Despite all that, Allyson still willingly agreed to have my mom move in with us.

The episode that epitomizes this dynamic best was one night early in our arrangement as my mom was retiring for the evening; I spontaneously asked her, "Mom, how long did it take you to really accept Allyson as my wife"?

I thought she would say maybe a year or possibly after the birth of Michael, our first child. But no, my mom quickly responded, "About ten years," and then she moved to her bedroom without breaking stride.

My mom unexpectedly passed away fifteen months after she moved in with us, and she came to know Allyson as a daughter. She would point to me and say, "You're my number one," and then point to Allyson and say, "You're my number two."

My wife gives of herself, and she is selfless. She cares about others and always thinks of their needs first above her own, whether it's her children, grandchildren, other family members, friends, or me. She is always there to help and wants the best for others. The ideal example of her thoughtfulness was allowing me to be me in following my heart during my quest of finding Paul.

Mothers are love, and that is my wife, Allyson!

There is no greater calling than to love and serve! And, mothers across the planet perform this act every single day. They are the unsung heroes of our world. Warrick Dunn's greatest gift to the world is honoring the love his mother provided to him and his siblings by serving the needs of other single moms through his Home for the Holidays charity.

What can you do to emulate a mother's love and make this world a better place?

One of the cool things about serving others is how it makes you feel. There is no greater joy in the world than knowing you've done something that makes another person's life better, and in the process, you become better. People who are struggling in life are often encouraged to volunteer for a charity because when they start to devalue themselves, the act of helping other people and bringing value to them can start to restore their belief in themselves.

When my USC teammates and I won a national championship, it was not because we played for ourselves; it is because we played for each other. That belief we had was rooted in the idea that every guy on the team had each other's back. We believed in each other as a group, which helped us to better believe in ourselves as individuals.

The power of belief can create miracles in your life, and there are several aspects that grow that belief. However, if there is one thing that rises above all else, it is easily love. Love yourself and love others. Go through life with love in your heart, and you will be able to move mountains. No small act of love is anything less than a miracle. It is truly the most powerful thing you can do as you move through the tunnel of life.

This journey through life can be made on autopilot, where you just meander from day to day with little purpose, or it can be an amazing adventure where you strive to live life like the miracle that it truly is. The fact that you made it to the end of the book suggests you want the latter and are searching—searching for better relationships, a career that matters, more money, improved health, or any number of other things that will lead to a fulfilled life.

Know that it's not too late to change. By simply turning the first page, you have already begun to move towards the life you have always imagined. There will be challenges while on your path, so be easy on yourself and take time to breathe. Remember to always be true to your authentic self and continue to trust and believe you deserve all that you desire, and your journey will lead to a life well lived.

GRATITUDE TO ALL

THERE IS NO SUCH THING as a bad experience in our growth and evolution as people, but this is true only if we are paying attention. Being conscious helps us avoid repeating the same mistake more than once and to learn from it, which moves us in the direction of our best self.

So, every encounter I've had during my lifetime, and even before I was born, has contributed to who I am in this very moment. They all add up—the positive and the perceived negative experiences—to create the current me.

Please understand, there have been people in my life, like my mom and dad, who have had significant personal influence. However, countless other individuals have, directly or indirectly, added a pinch of this or a pinch of that to help create the whole Paul.

Therefore, I would like to thank the people I've known well over the years, those I've only recently been acquainted with, and even those I may have never met. All of you have allowed me to put pen to paper to write this book, which has been a tremendous personal accomplishment.

I have immense gratitude to all of you for playing a role in my life and development.

Thank you all!

—Paul McDonald

ENDNOTES

1   Augustyn, Adam, "Marta." *Encyclopædia Britannica*.
    Encyclopædia Britannica, inc. Accessed September 6, 2021.
    https://www.britannica.com/biography/Marta.

2   Valls, Miuda, "Brazil's Marta Broke down Barriers to
    Become One of Football's Best Players." *CGTN America*,
    America.cgtn.com, August 13, 2019. https://america.cgtn.
    com/2019/08/11/brazils-marta-broke-down-barriers-to-
    become-one-of-footballs-best-players

3   Ibid.

4   Ibid.

5   Freeborn, Jeremy, "Carey Price," *The Canadian Encyclopedia*,
    Thecanadianencyclopedia.ca., March 16, 2017, https://www.
    thecanadianencyclopedia.ca/en/article/carey-price.

6   "Price and Riggle Prank Fans in Las Vegas," *YouTube*,
    YouTube, June 24, 2015, Video, https://www.youtube.com/
    watch?v=HBqtNIVCuoQ.

7   Wahl, Grant, "Ahead of His Class Ohio High School Junior LeBron James Is so Good That He's Already Being Mentioned as the Heir to Air Jordan - Sports Illustrated Vault," Sports Illustrated Vault, SI.com, February 18, 2002, https://vault.si.com/vault/2002/02/18/ahead-of-his-class-ohio-high-school-junior-lebron-james-is-so-good-that-hes-already-being-mentioned-as-the-heir-to-air-jordan.

8   Ibid.

9   Saslow, Eli, "Lost Stories Of LeBron, Part 1," *ESPN*, ESPN Internet Ventures, October 17, 2013, https://www.espn.com/nba/story/_/id/9825052/how-lebron-james-life-changed-fourth-grade-espn-magazine.

10 Ibid.

11 Emily Deruy and National Journal, "LeBron James Will Give College Scholarships to Thousands of Students," *The Atlantic*, Atlantic Media Company, August 17, 2015, https://www.theatlantic.com/politics/archive/2015/08/lebron-james-will-give-college-scholarships-to-thousands-of-students/432579/.

12 Davis, Scott, "LeBron James' Commitment to Send Kids from His School to College Could One Day Reach over $100 Million," *Business Insider*, Business Insider, July 31,

13 Norwood, Robyn, "A Sorry Chapter," *Los Angeles Times*, Latimes.com, October 17, 1997, https://www.latimes.com/archives/la-xpm-1997-oct-17-sp-43652-story.html.

14 Jenks, Jayson, "Pete Carroll's Failures: How Losing Has Defined Winning for the Seattle Seahawks Coach," *The Seattle Times*, The Seattle Times Company, October 30, 2015, https://www.seattletimes.com/sports/seahawks/pete-carrolls-failures-how-losing-has-defined-winning-for-the-seattle-seahawks-coach/.

15 Wikipedia, s.v. "Caron Butler," Wikimedia Foundation, last modified August 27, 2021, https://en.wikipedia.org/wiki/ Caron_Butler.

16 Butler, Caron, and Steve Springer, *Tuff Juice: My Journey from the Streets to the NBA* (Guilford, CT: Lyons Press, 2016).

17 Ibid.

18 Ibid.

19 Ruiz, Don Miguel. *The Four Agreements: A Practical Guide to Personal Freedom.* (California: Amber-Allen Publishing, 1997).

20 Tolle, Eckhart. *A New Earth: Awakening to Your Life's Purpose.* London, UK: Penguin Books, 2018.

21 Papale, Vince, and Chad Millman. *Invincible: My Journey from Fan to NFL Team Captain.* (New York, New York: Hyperion, 2006).

22 Ibid.

23 Ibid.

24 Norris, Luke, "What Kobe Bryant Did after Putting up Four Airballs Against the Utah Jazz in 1997 Was Pure 'Mamba Mentality,'" *Sportscasting*, Sportscasting.com, August 24, 2020, https://www.sportscasting.com/what-kobe-bryant-did- after-putting-up-four-airballs-against-the-utah-jazz-in-1997- was-pure-mamba-mentality/.

25 Ibid.

26 Astramskas, David, "(1997) Rookie Kobe Bryant Shoots 4 Airballs vs the Jazz in THE WCSF." *Ballislife.com.* Accessed September 6, 2021, https://ballislife.com/kobe-airball- jazz-97/.

27 Norris, Luke, "What Kobe Bryant Did after Putting up Four Airballs Against the Utah Jazz in 1997 Was Pure 'Mamba Mentality,'" *Sportscasting*, Sportscasting.com, August 24, 2020, https://www.sportscasting.com/what-kobe-bryant-did-after-putting-up-four-airballs-against-the-utah-jazz-in-1997-was-pure-mamba-mentality/.

28 NBA. "Kobe Bryant No.8 & No.24 Jersey Retirement In Los Angeles," *YouTube*, YouTube, December 18, 2017, Video, 13:26, https://www.youtube.com/watch?v=d1hs-JI_yBE.

29 Wikipedia, s.v. "Andre Iguodala," Wikimedia Foundation, last modified September 5, 2021. https://en.wikipedia.org/wiki/Andre_Iguodala.

30 Stock, Matthew, "Andre Iguodala's Journey from Starter to Sixth Man—to Finals MVP," *WBUR*, Wbur.org, June 28, 2019, https://www.wbur.org/onlyagame/2019/06/28/andre-iguodala-warriors-lebron-curry.

31 Ibid.

32 Taylor, Derrick Bryson, "Who Were the Freedom Riders?" *The New York Times*, Nytimes.com, July 18, 2020, https://www.nytimes.com/2020/07/18/us/politics/freedom-riders-john-lewis-work.html.

33 Frazier, Stephen. "John Lewis: 'I Thought I Was Going to Die,'" *CNN*, Edition.cnn.com, May 10, 2001, https://edition.cnn.com/2001/US/05/10/access.lewis.freedom.rides/.

34 Zinn, Brad, Monique Calello, and Ayano Nagaishi, "Hundreds Eventually Joined the Freedom Rides Movement. These Are the 13 Who Started It All," *USA Today*. Gannett Satellite Information Network, June 1, 2021, https://www.usatoday.com/story/news/nation/2021/06/01/original-freedom-riders-members-john-lewis-charles-person-1961/7490470002/.

35 Kragen, Pam. "San Diego-Raised Double-Amputee Makes History at Ironman World in Hawaii." *San Diego Union-Tribune*, Sandiegouniontribune.com, October 16, 2019. https://www.sandiegouniontribune.com/news/story/2019-10-15/san-diego-raised-double-amputee-makes-history-at-ironman-world-in-hawaii.

36 Sewell, Roderick, interview by Paul McDonald and Jack Baric, August, 2019.

37 Jackson, Marian, interview by Paul McDonald and Jack Baric, August, 2019.

38 The remainder of the story about Roderick Sewell is based on interviews with Roderick Sewell and his mother, Marian Jackson, in August of 2019 by Paul McDonald and Jack Baric.

39 Siddique, Haroon, "How Cori 'Coco' Gauff Made Her Fairytale Wimbledon Debut," *The Guardian*. Guardian News and Media, July 2, 2019, https://www.theguardian.com/sport/2019/jul/01/wimbledon-coco-gauff-fairytale-debut-venus-williams.

40 Ubha, Ravi, "Cori 'Coco' Gauff, 15, Loses at Wimbledon to End Magical Run," *CNN*, Cnn.com, July 9, 2019, https://www.cnn.com/2019/07/08/sport/coco-gauff-halep-wimbledon-tennis-spt-intl/index.html.

41 Bumbaca, Chris, "Coco Gauff Reveals She Almost Walked Away from Tennis While Dealing with Depression," *Behind the Racquet quoted in USA Today*, Gannett Satellite Information Network, April 16, 2020, https://www.usatoday.com/story/sports/tennis/2020/04/16/coco-gauff-opens-up-dealing-depression-expectations/5143341002/.

42 Ibid.

43 Ibid.

44 Ibid.

45　"Survey Finds Half of Girls Feel Paralyzed by the Fear of Failure during Puberty," *Procter & Gamble News*, August 16, 2017, https://news.pg.com/news-releases/news-details/2017/Survey-Finds-Half-of-Girls-Feel-Paralyzed-by-the-Fear-of-Failure-during-Puberty1-New-Always-LikeAGirl-Video-Aims-to-Change-This-and-Encourages-Girls-Everywhere-to-Keep-Going-LikeAGirl/default.aspx.

46　Dispenza, Joe, and Gregg Braden. *Becoming Supernatural: How Common People Are Doing the Uncommon*. Carlsbad, CA: Hay House, Inc., 2019.

47　"Your Brain on Imagination: It's a Lot like Reality, Study Shows," *ScienceDaily*, Sciencedaily.com, December 10, 2018, https://www.sciencedaily.com/releases/2018/12/181210144943.htm.

48　Ibid.

49　Wikipedia "Kevin Love," Wikimedia Foundation, last modified August 11, 2021, https://en.wikipedia.org/wiki/Kevin_Love.

50　Love, Kevin, "Everyone Is Going Through Something," *The Players' Tribune*. the playerstribune.com, March 6, 2021, https://www.theplayerstribune.com/articles/kevin-love-everyone-is-going-through-something.

51　Ibid.

52　Ibid.

53　Smith, Doug, "Raptors' DeRozan Hopes Honest Talk on Depression Helps Others," *Toronto Star*, thestar.com, February 25, 2018, https://www.thestar.com/sports/raptors/2018/02/25/raptors-derozan-hopes-honest-talk-on-depression-helps-others.html.

54　Rosario, Jason, "Dear Men: Featuring Kevin Love," *The Lives of Men*. Accessed September 7, 2021, Video, 5:28, http://www.thelivesofmen.com/watch.

55 Ibid., 5:31.

56 Bodo, Peter, "Simona Halep—Much-Loved, Often-Tormented—Must Fight Harder than Ever," *Tennis*, Tennis.com, May 2, 2018, https://www.tennis.com/news/articles/simona-halep-much-loved-often-tormented-must-fight-harder-than-ever.

57 Thomas, Louisa, "The Particular Drama of Simona Halep," *The New Yorker*, Newyorker.com, May 29, 2019, https://www.newyorker.com/culture/persons-of-interest/the-particular-drama-of-simona-halep.

58 Ibid

59 Cronin, Matt, "'Ashamed' Halep Had to Improve Attitude to Win Back Coach Cahill," *Tennis*, Tennis.com, June 6, 2017, https://www.tennis.com/news/articles/ashamed-halep-had-to-improve-attitude-to-win-back-coach-cahill.

60 Ibid.

61 Thomas, Louisa, "The Particular Drama of Simona Halep," *The New Yorker*, May 29, 2019, https://www.newyorker.com/culture/persons-of-interest/the-particular-drama-of-simona-halep.

62 Ibid.

63 Isaacson, Melissa, "Chasing Perfection: No. 1 Halep into Quarterfinals," *BNP Paribas Open*, March 13, 2018, https://bnpparibasopen.com/news/chasing-perfection-no-1-halep-into-quarterfinals/.

64 BNP Paribas Open. "BNP Paribas Open 2018: Simona HALEP 3R Press Conference," *YouTube*, YouTube, March 12, 2018, Video, 5:24, https://www.youtube.com/watch?v=EP4zPetvcvo.

65 Benjamin, Cody, "French Open 2018 Women's Final Result: Simona Halep Topples Sloane Stephens for First Grand Slam," *CBSSports.com*, CBS Sports, June 9, 2018. https://www.cbssports.com/tennis/news/french-open-2018-womens-final-result-simona-halep-topples-sloane-stephens-for-first-grand-slam/.

66 Thomas, Louisa, "The Particular Drama of Simona Halep," *The New Yorker*, May 29, 2019, https://www.newyorker.com/culture/persons-of-interest/the-particular-drama-of-simona-halep.

67 Wikipedia, s.v. "Armando Galarraga," Wikimedia Foundation, last modified July 29, 2021, https://en.wikipedia.org/wiki/Armando_Galarraga.

68 Wikipedia, s.v. "Armando Galarraga's near-Perfect Game," Wikimedia Foundation, last modified August 9, 2021, https://en.wikipedia.org/wiki/Armando_Galarraga%27s_near-perfect_game

69 Snyder, Matt, "Ex-Tigers Pitcher Armando Galarraga Wants MLB to Recognize 2010 Perfect Game, Overturn Blown Call," *CBSSports.com*, CBS Sports, May 12, 2020, https://www.cbssports.com/mlb/news/ex-tigers-pitcher-armando-galarraga-wants-mlb-to-recognize-2010-perfect-game-overturn-blown-call/.

70 Snyder, Matt, "Ex-Tigers Pitcher Armando Galarraga Wants MLB to Recognize 2010 Perfect Game, Overturn Blown Call," *CBSSports.com*, CBS Sports, May 12, 2020, https://www.cbssports.com/mlb/news/ex-tigers-pitcher-armando-galarraga-wants-mlb-to-recognize-2010-perfect-game-overturn-blown-call/.

71 Nelson, Amy K, "From the Archives: Blown Call in Armando Galarraga's'S Perfect Game Still Haunts Umpire Jim Joyce," *ESPN*, ESPN Internet Ventures, June 2, 2020, https://www.espn.com/espn/otl/news/story?id=5993137.

72 Wikipedia, s.v. "James Jones (Wide Receiver)," Wikimedia Foundation, August 1, 2021, https://en.wikipedia.org/wiki/James_Jones_(wide_receiver).

73 Beisner, Michelle, "James Jones: Full Circle," *ESPN*, ESPN Internet Ventures, December 20, 2015, Video, 1:34, https://www.espn.com/video/clip?id=14404735.

74 Organization, and ImageObject. "James Jones' Journey from Homeless Childhood to Chargers WR." James Jones' Journey from Homeless Childhood to Chargers WR, May 18, 2018. https://www.chargers.com/news/james-jones-journey-from-homeless-childhood-to-chargers-wr-134461.

75 Demovsky, Rob, "Packers' Top Plays: Favre-Rison In SBXXXI," *ESPN*, ESPN Internet Ventures, July 8, 2014, https://www.espn.com/blog/nflnation/post/_/id/130749/packers-top-play-favre-rison-in-sbxxxi.

76 Ibid.

77 Wilczek, Frank, "Einstein's Parable of Quantum Insanity," *Scientific American,* Scientific American.com, Scientific American, September 23, 2015, https://www.scientificamerican.com/article/einstein-s-parable-of-quantum-insanity/.

78 ABC news. ABC News Network, July 6, 2015, Video 1:01, https://abcnews.go.com/Entertainment/2015-fifa-womens-world-cup-carli-lloyd-visualized/story?id=32249479.

79 Magowan, Alistair, "Women's World Cup: USA 5–2 Japan." *BBC Sport*, BBC, July 6, 2015, https://www.bbc.com/sport/football/33085994

80 FIFA TV. "USA Reaction—Post Match Press Conference—CARLI LLOYD & Jill ELLIS (USA)," *YouTube*, YouTube, July 5, 2015, Video, 6:36, https://www.youtube.com/watch?v=5Nx-hBlg8w0&t=397s.

81 Begley, Sharon, "The Brain: How the Brain Rewires Itself," *Time*, Time Inc., January 19, 2007, http://content.time.com/ time/magazine/article/0,9171,1580438,00.html.

82 FIFA TV. "USA Reaction—Post Match Press Conference— CARLI LLOYD & Jill ELLIS (USA)." *YouTube*, YouTube, July 5, 2015, Video, 6:59, https://www.youtube.com/ watch?v=5Nx-hBlg8w0&t=397s.

83 Holiday, Ryan, "How a Buddhist Baseball Player Cleared His Mind—and Made History," *Next Big Idea Club*, October 3, 2019, https://nextbigideaclub.com/magazine/buddhist-baseball-player-cleared-mind-made-history/22470/.

84 Robson, Dan, "Shawn Green Talks Tee-Time and Zen Philosophy," *Toronto Star*, thestar.com June 10, 2011, https:// www.thestar.com/sports/baseball/2011/06/10/shawn_ green_talks_teetime_and_zen_philosophy.html.

85 Green, Shawn, and Gordon McAlpine, *The Way Of Baseball: Finding Stillness at 95 Mph* (New York: Simon & Schuster Paperbacks, 2012).

86 Simon, Andrew, "The Day Shawn Green Went Wild at the Plate," MLB.com, MLB, May 22, 2020, https://www.mlb.com/ news/shawn-green-four-home-run-game-records

87 Green, Shawn, and Gordon McAlpine. *The Way Of Baseball: Finding Stillness at 95 Mph* (New York: Simon & Schuster Paperbacks, 2012).

88 Ibid.

89 Holiday, Ryan, "How a Buddhist Baseball Player Cleared His Mind—and Made History." *Next Big Idea Club*. October 3, 2019, https://nextbigideaclub.com/magazine/buddhist-baseball-player-cleared-mind-made-history/22470/.

90 McKenna, Henry, "15-Year-Old Coco Gauff Had a Classy Response after Upsetting Venus Williams at Wimbledon," *Behind the Racquet quoted in USA Today*. Gannett Satellite Information Network, July 1, 2019, https://ftw.usatoday. com/2019/07/coco-gauff-beats-venus-williams-wimbledon.

91 Ibid.

92 Negley, Cassandra, "Coco Gauff Says She Struggled with Depression, Nearly Took Year off Before Wimbledon Stardom," Yahoo! Yahoo!, April 16, 2020, https://www.yahoo. com/now/coco-gauff-says-she-struggled-with-depression-nearly-took-year-off-before-wimbledon-breakout-210923860. html.

93 Tung, Liz, "Your Brain on Gratitude: How a Neuroscientist Used His Research to Heal from Grief," *WHYY.org*, WHYY, November 21, 2019, https://whyy.org/segments/your-brain-on-gratitude-how-a-neuroscientist-used-his-research-to-heal-from-grief/.

94 Wong, Y. Joel, Jesse Owen, Nicole T. Gabana, Joshua W. Brown, Sydney McInnis, Paul Toth, and Lynn Gilman (2018), "Does Gratitude Writing Improve the Mental Health of Psychotherapy Clients? Evidence from a Randomized Controlled Trial," *Psychotherapy Research*, 28:2, 192-202, DOI: https://www.tandfonline.com/doi/abs/10.1080/1050330 7.2016.1169332.

95 Wikipedia, s.v. "Alex Smith." Wikimedia Foundation, last modified September 5, 2021, https://en.wikipedia.org/wiki/ Alex_Smith#Professional_football_career

96 Ibid.

97 Ibid.

98 Corbett, Jim, "From Bench, Alex Smith Becomes Colin Kaepernick's Mentor," *USA Today*, Gannett Satellite Information Network, January 28, 2013, https://www.usatoday.com/story/sports/nfl/niners/2013/01/28/49ers-alex-smith-coaching-kaepernick/1872585/.

99 Wikipedia, s.v. "Alex Smith," Wikimedia Foundation, last modified September 5, 2021, https://en.wikipedia.org/wiki/Alex_Smith#Professional_football_career.

100 Homler, Ryan, "Patrick Mahomes Calls Alex Smith a 'Special Human Being,'" *NBC Sports Washington*, October 11, 2020, https://www.nbcsports.com/washington/football-team/patrick-mahomes-calls-his-mentor-alex-smith-special-human-being.

101 Mullainathan, Sendhil, and Eldar Shafir. *Scarcity: Why Having Too Little Means So Much* (New York: Picador, Henry Holt and Company, 2014).

102) "Abundance Noun - DEFINITION, PICTURES, Pronunciation and Usage Notes: Oxford ADVANCED American Dictionary at Oxfordlearnersdictionaries.com." abundance noun - Definition, pictures, pronunciation and usage notes | Oxford Advanced American Dictionary at OxfordLearnersDictionaries.com. Accessed September 20, 2021. https://www.oxfordlearnersdictionaries.com/us/definition/american_english/abundance#:~:text=noun-,noun,abundance%20of%20caf%C3%A9s%20and%20restaurants.

103 Wikipedia, s.v. "Alex Smith." Wikimedia Foundation, last modified September 5, 2021, https://en.wikipedia.org/wiki/Alex_Smith#Professional_football_career

104 Ibid.

105 "Project 11 | Watch ESPN." ESPN. ESPN Internet Ventures. Accessed September 20, 2021, Video, 3:23, https://www.espn.com/espnplus/player/_/id/69b74e6d-3717-45db-9f87-6b09ee87541c.

106 Ibid, 22:06.

107 Ibid, 28:45

108 Ibid, 29:40.

109 Ibid, 36:04.

110 Ibid, 38:34.

111 ESPN. "Alex Smith Reveals Details of Recovery, Future NFL Plans | SC with SVP." *YouTube*, YouTube, April 29, 2020 Video, 6:03, https://www.youtube.com/watch?v=QiHfP4iPDng.

112 Auriemma, Geno, "Body Language Matters—Geno Auriemma on Body Language and the Type of Players He Recruits," *NCAA.com*, YouTube, March 17, 2017, Video, 1:48, https://www.youtube.com/watch?v=tp4mIONS51E.

113 Wikipedia, s.v. "Geno Auriemma," Wikimedia Foundation, last modified August 26, 2021, https://en.wikipedia.org/wiki/Geno_Auriemma.

114 Auriemma, Geno, "Body Language Matters—Geno Auriemma on Body Language and the Type of Players He Recruits," NCAA.com, YouTube, March 17, 2017, Video, 0.01, 0.50, 2:26, https://www.youtube.com/watch?v=tp4mIONS51E.

115 "In First OT National Title Game, Buckeyes Prevail," *ESPN*, ESPN Internet Ventures, January 3, 2003, https://www.espn.com/college-football/recap/_/gameId/230032390.

116 Wikipedia s.v, "Maurice Clarett," Wikimedia Foundation, last modified June 20, 2021, https://en.wikipedia.org/wiki/Maurice_Clarett#Arrests_and_convictions.

117 Associated Press. "Clarett Receives Prison Sentence," *Deseret News*. Deseret.com, September 19, 2006, https://www.deseret.com/2006/9/19/19974889/clarett-receives-prison-sentence.

118 Clarett, Maurice, Bob Eckhart, and Jim Tressel, *One and Done: How My Life Started When My Football Career Ended* (Columbus, OH: Maurice Clarett and Bob Eckhart, 2019).

119 Ibid.

120 Today Show. "Maurice Clarett Shares Story of Redemption in Book 'One and Done,'" *3rd Hour Today, Motivational Monday*,TODAY.com. January 26, 2020, Video, 1:11, https://www.today.com/video/maurice-clarett-shares-story-of-redemption-in-book-one-and-done-76099653901.

121 Ibid., 2:29.

122 Ibid., 4:53.

123 Ibid., 1:58.

124 Rittenberg, Adam, "Inside the Latest Chapter of Former Ohio State Star Maurice Clarett's Life Turnaround," *ESPN*, ESPN Internet Ventures, May 12, 2020, https://www.espn.com/college-football/story/_/id/28490590/inside-latest-chapter-former-ohio-state-star-maurice-clarett-life-turnaround.

125 Clarett, Maurice, Bob Eckhart, and Jim Tressel, *One and Done: How My Life Started When My Football Career Ended* (Columbus, OH: Maurice Clarett and Bob Eckhart, 2019).

126 Wikipedia, s.v. "2019 WNBA Finals," Wikimedia Foundation, last modified August 9, 2021, https://en.wikipedia.org/wiki/2019_WNBA_Finals.

127 Ibid.

128 Ellentuck, Matt, "Elena Delle Donne's WNBA Finals Run Cements Her as One of the Best Ever," *SBNation*, SBNation.com, October 11, 2019, https://www.sbnation.com/wnba/2019/10/11/20909445/elena-delle-donne-wnba-finals-washington-mystics-injuries-back-nose-knees.

129 Patrick, Dick, "After Time out, Play Resumes," *USA Today*, PressReader.com, November 30, 2009, https://www.pressreader.com/usa/usa-today-international-editi on/20091130/281779920218927.

130 Hays, Graham, "Finding Her Way Back Home," *ESPNW*. ESPN Internet Ventures. Accessed September 8, 2021, http://www.espn.com/espn/eticket/story?page=elenaDonne.

131 Patrick, Dick, "After Time out, Play Resumes." *USA Today*, PressReader.com, November 30, 2009. https://www.pressreader.com/usa/usa-today-international-editi on/20091130/281779920218927.

132 Hays, Graham, "Finding Her Way Back Home," *ESPNW*. ESPN Internet Ventures. Accessed September 8, 2021. http://www.espn.com/espn/eticket/story?page=elenaDonne.

133 Fox, Ken, "For WNBA Star Delle Donne, Family Comes First," *The Elkhart Truth*, Elkharttruth.com, March 21, 2017. https://www.elkharttruth.com/sports/for-wnba-star-delle-donne-family-comes-first/article_f7fee32d-1615-541b-9cf4-fddea69be5f5.html.

134 Ibid.

135 Hawkins, David R., *Power vs. Force* (Hay House Inc., 2014).

136 Ibid.

137 Ibid.

138 Lynch, David, "Liverpool, Premier League champions! 30-Year Title Drought Over After Man City Fail to Beat Chelsea," *Evening Standard*, Standard.co.uk.com, June 25, 2020, https://www.standard.co.uk/sport/football/liverpool-fc-premier-league-champions-win-the-title-30-years-a4480111.html.

139 Median income by country 2021. Accessed September 8, 2021, https://worldpopulationreview.com/country-rankings/median-income-by-country

140 Spotrac.com, s.v. "Sadio Mane," Spotrac.com. Accessed September 8, 2021. https://www.spotrac.com/epl/liverpool-fc/sadio-mane-22847/.

141 Joe, Dada, "'I Won't Use My Money to Buy Ferrari, I Will Help My People' - Sadio Mane Speaks," *Nsemwoha*, Nsemwoha.com, October 13, 2019, https://www.nsemwoha.com/i-wont-use-my-money-to-buy-ferrari-i-will-help-my-people-sadio-mane-speaks/.

142 Ibid.

143 Ibid.

144 Wikipedia, s.v. "Warrick Dunn," Wikimedia Foundation, last modified August 28, 2021, https://en.wikipedia.org/wiki/Warrick_Dunn.

145 Welch, Monique, "Former Buc Warrick Dunn Surprises St. Pete Single Mother with New Home," *Tampa Bay Times*, Tampabay.com, October 29, 2019, https://www.tampabay.com/news/st-petersburg/2019/10/15/former-buc-warrick-dunn-surprises-st-pete-single-mother-with-new-home/.

146 "Homes for the Holidays," Warrick Dunn Charities, August 24, 2021, https://wdc.org/homes-for-the-holidays/.

147 Ibid.

148 Welch, Monique, "Former Buc Warrick Dunn Surprises St. Pete Single Mother with New Home," *Tampa Bay Times*, Tampabay.com, October 29, 2019, https://www.tampabay.com/news/st-petersburg/2019/10/15/former-buc-warrick-dunn-surprises-st-pete-single-mother-with-new-home/.

149 Bynum, Georgia, "Roger Federer: Tennis Player and Humanitarian," *BORGEN Magazine, borgenmagazine.com*, May 20, 2021, https://www.borgenmagazine.com/roger-federer/.

9TH STRING TO
THE NFL

A STORY YOUR AUDIENCE
WILL LOVE TO HEAR

WHEN PAUL MCDONALD walked onto the USC campus as a freshman quarterback he was ninth on the depth chart. He started as a 9th stringer! To make matters worse, Vince Evans, the Trojans starting quarterback was stronger, faster, bigger, and could throw the ball waaaaay further than Paul. "If that is what it means to be a quarterback at USC, I have no chance," raced through Paul's mind.

Paul went from this humble position at USC to becoming a starter on the Trojans national championship football team, an All-American quarterback, and an eight year career in the NFL.

How did Paul do it? He discovered his own path to becoming the best quarterback he could be instead of someone else's version of one. Paul spent countless hours in the film room to elevate himself into being a top level cerebral quarterback, which led him to Rose Bowl triumphs and the opportunity to play in the NFL for the Cleveland Browns and Dallas Cowboys.

Paul's journey provided the thrill of running through NFL stadiums, but when his football career ended he was forced to make the rough transition to sitting in a corporate office cubicle. This led to some unhappy times for Paul until he discovered the secrets of diving inward to find the things in life that he truly loved, even while holding the same job he previously disliked. His story provides great hope to anyone struggling with being at a place in life that lacks purpose and joy.

Paul McDonald's stories on finding an authentic path to a better life will provide your event with an inspirational message that your audience will never forget.

To book Paul to speak at your event:

Please send an email to speakers@gamechangenation.com

EMPOWERMENT THROUGH SPORTS

Thru the Tunnel authors Paul McDonald and Jack Baric are the co-founders of GameChange, a media company that partners with athletes, coaches, and mind/body/spirit experts to create inspirational sports and personal empowerment content that is designed to help its audience enjoy a more successful and joyful life.

GameChange is creating a community of positive individuals who love sports, strive to be better, and enjoy helping others do the same. The company has built GameChangeNation.com, a place where people gather to elevate themselves and each other. The website distributes free daily content in the form of videos, podcasts, blogs, and graphics. It also provides numerous interactive opportunities.

In addition to the free content, GameChangeNation.com includes various mind/body/spirit classes that are available for subscription. Anyone purchasing a copy of *Thru the Tunnel* will receive a free basic subscription, which includes a 12 episode class that is led by Paul.

Please email classcode@gamechangenation.com to receive a free promo code for Paul's class.

PLEASE JOIN GAMECHANGENATION!

GAMECHANGE

PERFECT FOR HIGH SCHOOL
AND CLUB TEAMS

GameChange, the company co-founded by *Thru the Tunnel* authors Paul McDonald and Jack Baric, has created a twelve-episode online class that blend the positive mindset principles found in the book with a program designed to position students as great candidates for college admissions. The GameChange website also provides coaches with private online rooms to post their own inspirational messages and information for their team.

The GameChange system is applicable for both students who hope to play college sports and those who can point to their high school career as a positive attribute on college applications. The program encourages students to reflect on how their personal experiences relate to the principles being taught and it features writing prompts matching the essay questions found on college applications.

GameChange also provides students the opportunity to submit their own stories for *Friday Night Writes*, a weekly blog about the student athlete experience, with the best stories bound together into a book.

Please email studentprogram@gamechangenation.com for more information on how your athletic program, team, or club can subscribe to GameChange for your student athletes.

CPSIA information can be obtained
at www.ICGtesting.com
Printed in the USA
LVHW040323190822
726312LV00003B/194